Better Homes and Gardens

PRUNING
& PLANTING
Beautiful Results

Roger Mann

MURDOCH BOOKS®

Sydney • London • Vancouver

CONTENTS

Pruning...4

Planting...18

Encyclopaedia of plants

Vines & climbers...27

Shrubs 39

Trees 85

Index 124

PRUNING

An English gardener once visited one of the famous temple gardens in Japan and asked the head gardener what was the secret of creating such beauty. The head gardener simply held up his pruning shears and smiled ...

THE POINT WAS WELL MADE—PRUNING is one of the essential activities of gardening. We think of it mainly in the context of woody plants—trees, shrubs, roses and the like—but whenever we snip off a dead flower for the sake of neatness, pinch back the shoots of a chrysanthemum to make it bushy or even mow the lawn, we are pruning. Pruning is simply the removal of some part of a plant in order to encourage it to grow the way we want it to. It calls for both artistry and skill; but so do most aspects of gardening. If you have carefully chosen your plants and cultivated them to the point where you are thinking of pruning, then pruning should hold no terrors for you.

Pruning can subtly alter the character of a garden. Here, judicious thinning of the dense pittosporums would reveal the graceful lines of the gum trees and allow in more light.

WHY PRUNE?

FIRST ASK YOURSELF WHY YOU WANT TO prune the plant at all, rather than simply let it grow untouched. There are a dozen reasons why you might decide to prune:

1 Taking out our own frustrations by hacking away at some poor defenceless plant. While this may be therapeutic, it rarely does much good for the plant. Don't prune if you are in a temper!

2 Controlling a plant's size. It is true that if the plant is given enough room to grow to its full size without being crowded, there will be no need to curtail its growth; but sometimes we deliberately plant a vigorous plant knowing we will have to keep it within bounds. Wisteria, for instance, will need to be controlled on any but the largest of pergolas.

3 Encouraging more or better flowers or fruit. This is why rose bushes and fruit trees are pruned more or less elaborately, and why we snip off dead flowers to keep a plant from wasting energy in unwanted seeds. Most pruning of flowering shrubs is directed to this end also. (Often unnecessarily: if a shrub is healthy and flowering abundantly, why prune it?)

4 Grooming a plant to keep it looking presentable. Usually all this involves is removing unsightly dead flowers or branches; sometimes we might go a little further and remove a shoot that is threatening to spoil the plant's symmetry. Mowing the lawn is grooming too.

5 Enhancing the plant's natural form. We might pinch the shoots of a naturally bushy plant such as lavender to keep it compact or, conversely, we might remove superfluous growth from a tree or shrub to open it out and

HOW A PLANT GROWS

Plant roots grow below ground, where they tap from the soil water and nutrients, which are carried up through the stems to the growing parts of the plants, the leaves, flowers and fruit. At the same time the sugars that the leaves prepare by means of photosynthesis are carried through the stems to the roots. Whether the stem in question is a trunk, a branch, a twig, or an actively growing shoot, it is essentially a tube conveying sap, and if you cut it off, you divert the sap and the plant's energy to some other stem, which will then grow more strongly.

A stem can be cut back to another, preferred stem or it can be cut back to a bud, from which a new stem will arise. On most plants buds can be seen as small nubs, either at the end of a stem (the terminal bud) or along the sides (the lateral buds). Lateral buds almost always grow in the axil ('armpit') of a leaf. Once a stem matures, the buds may disappear beneath the bark, to lie dormant (they are called latent buds) until pruning or injury removes the growth above them and provokes them into growth.

When you cut a stem back, you remove the terminal bud, forcing the lateral buds into growth to make side shoots. This usually makes the plant bushier. Conversely, you might choose to pinch back side shoots, diverting the plant's energy into the terminal bud to make the branch grow longer. And by cutting back hard into old wood, you may also force latent buds into growth.

The way you prune a plant depends on the sort of growth that will come from each bud. If you are training a climbing rose, for instance, you might remove the ends of the long shoots to force the side shoots that will bear the flowers; if you are training a young tree to grow tall, you might well shorten the side shoots to encourage the main shoot (the leader) to grow faster; or if you are faced with a straggly plant you might cut into the old wood to force latent buds to shoot, but take all care with this method—most conifers and many Australian plants won't respond to this treatment. This may sound discouragingly complex and technical but with the plant before you, it is usually easy to see how its stems and buds will grow, and with that knowledge you will be able to see how to prune them to achieve whatever result you may want.

Terminal bud

Lateral buds

Internode

Leaf scar

Leaf

Third year's growth starts here

Terminal bud

Latent bud

Spur

Second year's growth starts here

First year's growth starts here

How not to prune! The cherry tree and purple plum were hanging over the footpath—but just cutting back has left ugly and unhealthy stumps. Better to cut back to junctions.

reveal the lines of its branches, an art at which the Japanese are masters. Or we might cut back the long shoots of a hibiscus, say, to encourage it to become more bushy and flowery, without actually trying to persuade it to grow in an artificial shape.

6 Creating a pleasing artificial form. Naturally, 'pleasing' in this context is in the eye of the beholder! Topiary, where plants are sheared into cones, balls or peacocks, is the extreme of artifice; but clipping a hedge, or training a tree or shrub espalier against a wall, also creates an artificial form.

7 Helping remedy damage, as when we remove limbs broken in a storm or cut out frost-killed or disease-infested shoots. Dead branches are not only unsightly, they often harbour disease or decay, and so it usually benefits the plant to remove them. Transplanting often involves unavoidable damage to roots, and so we cut back the top growth in order to bring the plant back into balance.

8 Rejuvenating an old, overgrown or neglected shrub that has become an unproductive mass of twiggy growth.

9 Letting in light and air. Sometimes this is done to a perfectly healthy tree (or large shrub)

which is casting more shade than we want. Other times we do it for the sake of the plant, to clean out branches and twigs that are depriving other branches of light. Most fruit tree pruning has this aim—to let the light through to the lower branches so that they will bear fruit low enough to be picked in comfort.

10 Encouraging a young tree to develop a strong, symmetrical framework of branches.

11 Correcting mistakes—other people's, naturally! Sometimes we are undoing the effects of previous bad pruning (the therapeutic-for-the-gardener variety); all too often, we are forced into continuous cutting back because some plant is outgrowing its allotted space, maybe encroaching on a path. (Pruning might not be the only remedy. Could you, for instance, re-align the path?)

Before you take out the pruning shears, look at your plant. If none of these reasons for pruning suggests itself, do you need to prune at all? Nature doesn't prune, after all, and you only have to come across a neglected rose bush smothered in flowers or an unpruned apple tree groaning under the weight of fruit to realise that the directions you find in books (including this one!) to 'prune after flowering' or 'cut back in winter' or whatever should be taken as meaning 'that's when and how to prune if you want to'. Your own temperament will play a part in the decision: a perfectionist will probably feel the need to do more pruning than someone whose approach to gardening is more relaxed. It's your garden—who is to say which way is right for you and your garden?

PRUNING TECHNIQUES

IF YOU DECIDE TO PRUNE, THERE ARE four basic techniques you can use, depending on what you want to achieve and the way the plant grows. These techniques—pinching, shearing, heading (or cutting) back and thinning—all start the same way, with the removal of any dead and obviously weak and sickly branches or shoots. Sometimes that is all that is needed. Take a critical look at your plant before proceeding further.

PINCHING
Pinching is the simplest pruning method. You simply pinch out the tip of a shoot while it is growing, taking the end of the shoot (with the terminal bud) and maybe a leaf or two. Whether you use your finger nails or shears is a matter of personal choice; either way, the result is to force

Pinching

Heading back

the lateral buds to start their growth. Repeated pinching will make many new shoots and give a compact bushy plant: lavender plants, and also petunia and marigold seedlings are pruned this way. Usually you will only need to pinch a plant twice, and you shouldn't pinch once the plant shows signs of wanting to flower and is large enough to do so. The side shoots of a young tree or grape vine can be pinched back to encourage the plant to put most of its energy into the terminal bud and thus to grow taller.

SHEARING
Shearing is like pinching on a more drastic scale: you clip the outer parts of the plant to an even surface, using a pair of hedge shears. Repeated shearing destroys the plant's natural form, but that may be what you want. Shearing a hedge is the most obvious example, but you might also want to shear back a groundcover planting to make it grow lower and more evenly or to remove a multitude of dead flowers. Shearing doesn't allow you to make your cuts precisely above a bud as you would normally, and the best plants for hedges and topiary are those that grow back no matter where you cut. Shearing is not suitable for plants with large leaves such as camellias—you will end up cutting a lot of the leaves in half, which can create an unpleasant sight. It is much better to trim these large-leaved plants by cutting back each shoot individually with secateurs.

Shearing

HEADING BACK
Heading back shortens a branch without removing it entirely and thus forces growth from one or more lateral buds. You might head back to reduce the size of the plant, to encourage growth from lower down where it will be stronger or more productive of flowers or fruit, or to remove a part of a branch that has been damaged. Always head back to a point from which growth will come—to another branch or to a bud—and consider whether that growth is likely to go in the direction you want. And don't leave stubs to rot! Usually, you will want to take out a few branches entirely, lest the plant end up making so many new branches that they crowd each other out.

Always go easy when heading back. You can always cut off more, but you can't stick branches back on. And remember that you may be removing fruiting or flowering wood.

THINNING
Thinning is the removal of whole stems, cutting them right back to their origin, with the aim of reducing the plant's bulk and bushiness but not making it any smaller. You might do this to let in more light and air, to reveal the lines of the branches or, by removing old and unproductive stems, to channel the plant's energies into younger and more productive ones.

Thinning

Often you will combine thinning and heading back, as in the pruning of bush roses where you cut out old branches and head back the rest.

CHOOSING A TECHNIQUE

EVERY PLANT IS DIFFERENT AND HOW you apply the basic techniques will vary from plant to plant, but there are some general principles to bear in mind for each class of plant.
♣TREES usually need some pruning when young to encourage them to develop into shapely adults, with well-spaced, symmetrical branches

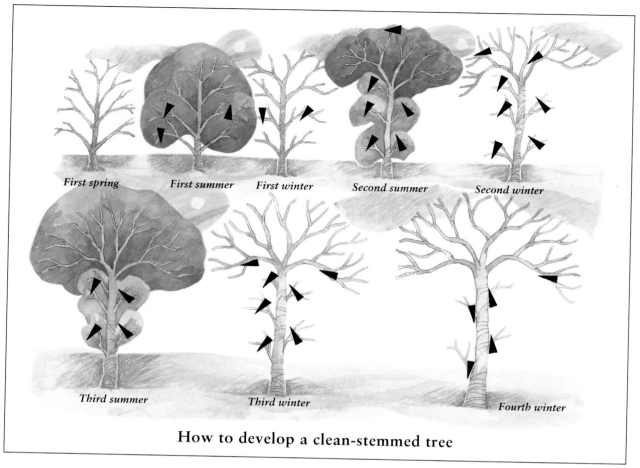

First spring   First summer   First winter   Second summer   Second winter

Third summer   Third winter   Fourth winter

How to develop a clean-stemmed tree

growing out wide from the main trunk—narrow, V-shaped crotches tend to be weak and may split when the tree reaches full size. If you have bought your tree bare-rooted (that is, without soil around its roots, the way roses are usually sold) or with its roots balled up in hessian, it will have lost roots when lifted from the nursery field and you should head back the branches about halfway to restore balance. If it has no branches (what nursery people and orchardists call a whip), you can shorten it by about a third, cutting back to a bud so that it will grow a new leader come spring, or you can leave it unpruned. Training a young tree is not a hasty business and it is best to take several years over the initial pruning. This is probably better than chopping a baby tree about.

An established tree usually needs only the removal of dead wood and the thinning out of overcrowded branches, especially where they are rubbing against each other and the bark is being chafed. But it is often desirable to thin out the branches to allow more light and air to reach the garden beneath. This is almost always better than trying to curtail the tree's size by hard cutting back. Go easy when pruning—ideally, your

activities should not be obvious. First cut out weaker branches and then any that are growing immediately above or below others. Then stand back and see how everything looks before you take any more. If a tree is branching too low, you can cut away the lowest branches so as to 'raise the crown', but it is better to do it over a couple of years than all at once. Some very desirable trees grow like overgrown shrubs, with several trunks and low branches—the deciduous magnolias and the silk tree (Albizia julibrissin),

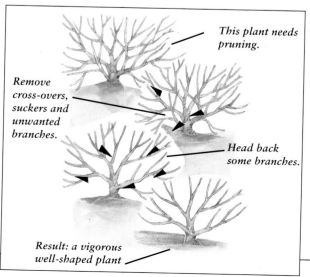

This plant needs pruning.

Remove cross-overs, suckers and unwanted branches.

Head back some branches.

Result: a vigorous well-shaped plant

Plant structure

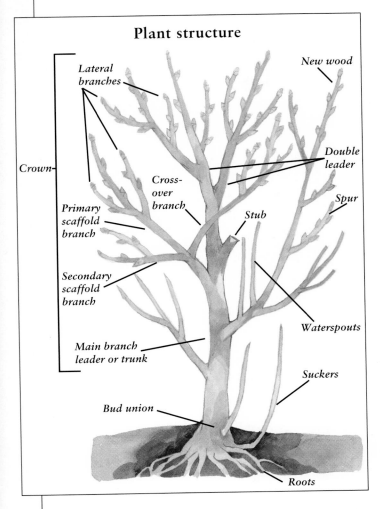

Lateral branches
New wood
Crown
Double leader
Cross-over branch
Spur
Primary scaffold branch
Stub
Secondary scaffold branch
Waterspouts
Main branch leader or trunk
Suckers
Bud union
Roots

♣GROUNDCOVERS are a very mixed group: some, such as ivy, are climbers that trail along the ground for want of something to climb up; some, such as hypericum and vinca, are spreading herbaceous perennials; while others are prostrate, spreading shrubs. The prostrate junipers and cotoneasters come into this category, and they need careful treatment at the edges of the planting, for instance where they encroach on a path. If you just trim them off, they will build up a hedge-like mass of growth, which looks dreadful. To preserve an irregular edge, you need to selectively take long branches back into the main mass, combining heading back with thinning. An occasional shearing or general heading back will keep all types of ground covers dense and low.

♣SHRUBS fall into two main groups: those that have several permanent branches growing from a single rootstock, like trees with only a vestigial trunk, and those that form clumps or thickets of more or less evenly sized stems growing straight from the ground. Shrubs with a single rootstock, such as daphne and most grevilleas, are usually headed back, although you might want to thin out the occasional weak or badly placed branch to keep them from becoming too bushy. On the other hand, thicket shrubs such as philadelphus, abelias and shrub roses are generally pruned by thinning, occasionally cutting a few of the oldest branches right to the ground to make way for younger ones. Large shrubs such as camellias and the bigger bottlebrushes can be trained as small, multi-stemmed trees (there is no hard and fast dividing line between a big shrub and a small tree) by removing the lowest branches, and this is often the best way to deal with them. Not all will take being severely headed back into bare wood to make them smaller and it may be better to begin pruning when they are still young and flexible.

for instance. You can remove the lowest branches if you want to walk or grow other plants underneath, and if you start early it is usually possible to train them to a single trunk by removing all but the strongest main stem. You then proceed as you would with a regular single-stemmed tree, but watch out for and remove any shoots that would grow up into further trunks. (You can also train many shrubs this way to create a standard, an effect which will result in a plant that looks like a floral lollipop. See page 58.)

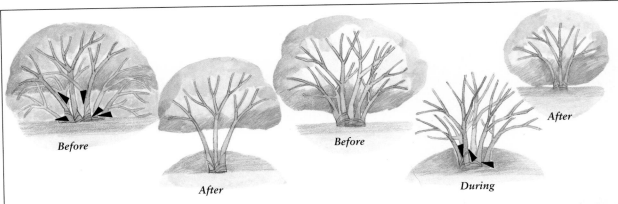

Before

After

Convert a multi-stemmed shrub to a small tree by removing lower limbs and excess stems.

Before

During

After

Renovate an overgrown shrub over three years—each winter cut to ground one-third of the oldest stems.

♣CONIFERS are cone-bearing plants that range from creeping groundcovers to the world's tallest timber trees. With few exceptions, they are evergreen and their leaves are needles: either long as in pines and cedars or short as in cypresses and junipers. They fall into two broad classes: those such as pines, cedars and firs that bear their branches in whorls, radiating out from the trunk or limbs like the spokes of a wheel, and those such as sequoias, cypresses and junipers that branch at random along the stem. This is not a commonly used distinction, but it is important when pruning, for while the random branchers have dormant buds all along their shoots so that you can cut anywhere and expect growth, the whorl branchers have buds only at the points where the whorls arise—at the tips or the bases of new shoots. If you cut between them, there will be no growth and the cut branch will die back: cut only to a lateral or, if you can see it clearly, to the cluster of buds that mark the base of a year's growth. (See the diagram below.)

Almost all the whorl branching conifers have a strongly dominant leading shoot that grows faster than the side branches: this gives young trees their characteristic conical appearance. (It often declines in vigour with maturity, which is why old pines and cypresses are flat topped.) Don't damage it, but if it is accidentally cut, tie the strongest branch from the top whorl to a vertical stake; with this assistance, it will

If a conifer loses its leading shoot, stake the strongest of the topmost branches upright to take its place.

become a new leader. Sometimes a tree will make two leaders. Remove the weaker to preserve the tree's symmetry. Random branchers have strong leaders too, although their dominance is slightly less obvious. You can hold the tree to a desired height by cutting the leader back, but then you will have to shorten side branches also to keep the tree in balance and prevent it from becoming flat topped. For a few years at least, you can thus hold the random branchers to about a third of their natural height, but eventually they become dumpy and unnatural looking. It is much better to clip them to a frankly artificial shape like a cone or pyramid— if that won't look ridiculous.

In fact, most conifers are naturally shapely, and if you choose a conifer to suit your situation, you should not need to prune. In any case, don't cut into bare wood—the dormant buds lose viability when the leaves finally fall and so it won't regrow. (*Taxus*, the English yew, and *Podocarpus*, the plum pines, are notable exceptions, which is one reason why yew is so valued for hedging and topiary.)

THE SURGEON'S ART: MAKING A PRUNING CUT

It may seem pedantic to insist that there is a right way and a wrong way to do the simple job of cutting off a piece of stem, but remember that a plant is a living thing and pruning is a kind of surgery from which it has to heal itself. Properly made cuts will heal quickly; bad ones will heal only slowly, if at all, and the open wounds will invite infection and decay.

Except in shearing, all cuts must be made either where the plant will grow or where, if it will not grow, it can heal itself. Usually this means to just above a bud (choose a lateral bud in the axil of a leaf on a growing stem or find a dormant bud on a leafless stem), just above another branch, or back to the main trunk or rootstock. If you leave a stub above a growing or healing point, it will die back and rot, and the rot can spread to the living tissue.

Random branching **Whorl branching**

Juniper *Pine* *Spruce*

Where to make cuts

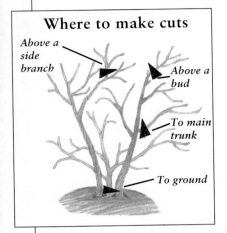

Above a side branch
Above a bud
To main trunk
To ground

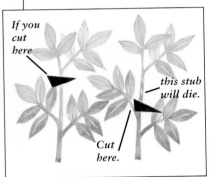

If you cut here
this stub will die.
Cut here.

Pruning cuts

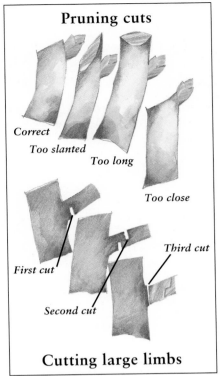

Correct
Too slanted
Too long
Too close
First cut
Second cut
Third cut

Cutting large limbs

The picture on the left shows the right way to hold secateurs—so that the flat blade bruises the part you cut off. In the picture on the right, the main part of the branch has been cut off (note how the bark tore) and now the stub is being trimmed close to the trunk.

As important as placing your cut correctly is making it cleanly; a ragged wound won't heal. This means that your tools must be sharp—send them off to be sharpened, or replace them with new, sharp ones.

WHEN TO PRUNE

A LOT OF MINOR PRUNING—PINCHING, removing dead wood, shortening that wayward branch—can in fact be done at almost any time you notice the need. But any major pruning of trees and shrubs is best done when the plant is dormant and can best cope with the shock. For most plants, this means in the winter; but there is a large class of plants (apples, philadelphus, weigelas, pears, shrub roses, poinsettias, azaleas, wisteria) that flower in spring on the previous summer's growth, and if you prune them in winter you will be cutting away their flowering wood. They should be pruned immediately the flowers are over, before new growth is properly underway. If you like, you can combine pruning with cutting flowers for the house, taking the branches that you plan to prune out, and finishing off the job when the rest of the flowers have fallen. Summer flowerers, on the other hand, mostly bloom on the current season's growth and can be pruned at any time from the end of autumn until they show signs of growth in spring. (In later chapters of the book, the class to which the plant belongs is noted.) Most trees grow very slowly towards the end of summer, and you can do any major thinning out then—it can be easier to judge what to take while a deciduous tree still has its leaves on.

SPECIAL TYPES OF PRUNING

STANDARDS

While the official difference between a tree and a shrub is that a tree has only one main stem and a shrub has several, it is possible to train many shrubs to grow on a relatively tall single stem, like small trees. Shrubs trained this way are called standards. The lollipop-like effect is best suited to a formal environment, and you probably won't want to dot standards around a casually designed garden.

There are two ways to create a standard. The most common method is to use the same process as for the initial training of a single-stemmed tree. Choose a single-stemmed plant if possible, otherwise start with a young plant, selecting the strongest branch as the leader. Head back the others and stake the leader, pinching back any side shoots it might develop. Then, when it has

ANNUALS & PERENNIALS

♣ *ANNUALS are usually pinched at planting out time to encourage them to grow more bushy and flowery. Regularly removing dead flowers prevents them setting seed, which is apt to bring flowering to a halt. You can just snip them off, but it's neater to trim the flower stalks back to new growth. If that is too tedious, just cut overgrown plants back halfway in mid-season and soon there will be fresh flowers.*

♣ *BULBS have their spent flowers removed, with as little foliage as possible, to prevent plants from diverting energy into seed when they should be concentrating on building themselves up for next year. Don't clear away the leaves until they have died down naturally.*

♣ *PERENNIALS (dahlias, chrysanthemums) may benefit from pinching in spring, but some do not. After bloom cut the spent flower stems well back; whether this will encourage further bloom depends on the species—experience will tell.*

reached the height you want, pinch its tip to force branches there and, when these have begun to develop, cut everything else away. The process may take two or three years, depending on how fast the plant grows naturally. In future years, at the usual pruning time, you head back the branches of the head as needed to keep it symmetrical and compact. Eventually, the main stem should become sturdy enough so that you can dispense with the stake, but don't be in too great a hurry. You can try this method with almost any shrub if you have the patience, but those that naturally tend to grow from one point are better choices than those that grow in thickets (such as oleanders), as they will resent being confined to a single stem and sucker constantly. Try camellias, hibiscus, buddleias, azaleas, bay trees, fuchsias, gardenias, raphiolepis, ixoras, abutilon, bougainvillea and wisteria for starters.

You can apply the same treatment to a bushy climber, training your leader around a stout stake and regularly pinching and heading back the head to keep it compact. The process is faster than with a shrub, but you'll have to keep the stake permanently in place. *Tecomaria capensis*, *Trachelospermum jasminoides* and *Solanum jasminoides* all lend themselves to being grown in this way, and I should think you could try it with *Sollya heterophylla* and some of the mandevilleas also—'Red Riding Hood' strikes me as sufficiently bushy.

The second method is to graft or bud the variety that is to form the head at the top of a

suitably tall, straight understock. This is how standard roses are created, and the method is also used for weeping standards. The grafting or budding procedure is as usual for the plant; the only problem (apart from getting hold of the understock in the first place) is that the swelling that usually develops over the years at graft unions can look most unnatural up in the air.

With any standard, you'll have to keep watch for suckers from the trunk or from the roots and rub them off as soon as they start up.

WEEPING STANDARDS

Weeping standards ideally should look like a graceful fountain. Roses are the commonest of the weeping standards, but birches, elms, cherries, grevilleas and even cedars can be trained this way. They are all normally produced by grafting a pendulous cultivar of the plant concerned to a long stem. Weeping standard grevilleas are made by grafting a prostrate variety such as 'Royal Mantle' to a stem of *Grevillea robusta*. Grafted plants are expensive to buy and the swelling that develops at graft unions can be unsightly. (To my mind, this ends up ruining the appearance of most grafted weeping cherries.) Grafted plants can also look very ungainly, like collapsed umbrellas, and their appearance can be greatly enhanced if you select a strong shoot and stake it upwards to give a bit of height to the crown. It's a pity that the nurseries don't do this, and it's not always easy if the plant is an 'advanced' one, with its branches already well developed and hanging down.

There is no reason why you cannot train a weeping plant from infancy on its own roots. Select a leader, keep it well staked and follow the usual procedures for creating a standard. It will, however, take longer than grafting. Pruning of these plants consists only of removing branches that interfere with the shape of the plant, at the usual pruning time for the species; once branches touch the ground, they should be tipped to clear it.

HEDGES

A hedge is a row of trees or shrubs (usually, but not always, of the one species) which are clipped or sheared to an even height and width. You can

The length of a standard is a matter of proportion. These lantanas look just right on stems a little less than a metre tall.

need to clip: simply plant a row of some attractive, low-branching shrub, a little more closely than usual, pinch the young growth a few times to ensure the plants will be bushy to the ground and let them grow into an informal hedge. All the pruning needed will be an occasional heading back to ensure the mass of greenery and flowers stays dense. Evergreens such as oleanders, hibiscus, *Camellia sasanqua,* azaleas or cotoneasters are the usual choice, but you could use densely branched deciduous shrubs such as shrub roses or flowering quinces if you prefer. Just make sure they aren't going to grow taller than you had in mind or you will have to spend many hours trimming the hedge.

A clipped hedge is a bit more trouble, but it does give you absolute control over the height (and perhaps more importantly, the width) of your hedge, and the formal, architectural lines that come with neat shearing can be very telling in a garden design; a neat wall of sheared green can be the best of all backdrops for a kaleidoscopic planting of flowers. The best plants are, naturally enough, those that can take regular shearing without complaining, such as cypresses, yew and privet (but in many areas of Australia privet is a noxious weed). However, if you are prepared to use secateurs rather than shears, so that you don't see half your leaves cut in half, you could use such large-leaved shrubs as camellias, bay trees or even azaleas. Just remember that clipping will probably remove much flowering wood—it is difficult to get both formal shape and a lavish display of flowers. And there is no need to think only in terms of more than head-height screens—low hedges of such plants as box, rosemary or lavender can make very effective dividers in the garden or can enclose

either shear to a geometrical form, with straight sides and a flat or rounded top, or have a less formal effect by simply shortening odd branches that grow too far. Hedges can be useful, making green enclosing walls with less sense of confinement than a fence or masonry wall would give. Choose the appropriate plant, and you can have your hedge at any height from ankle high to well over your head.

The traditional use of hedges to enclose fields and paddocks has never been common in Australia—we have always relied more on wire fences—and these days their main use is in gardens. They can be substitutes for fences where these are frowned on by local councils or used as screens for privacy. The original reason for clipping them was to make them dense enough to keep people out and animals in, but if all we want is to block unwanted vision, there is no

Trimming a hedge

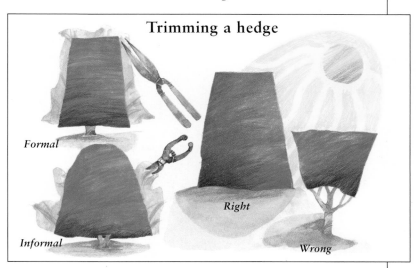

Formal

Informal

Right

Wrong

plants in the manner of old French or Italian gardens. (You'll find suggestions for good hedging species throughout the later chapters.)

Start by planting closer than you would otherwise, at about half the usual spacing for the species (in other words, about half the spread an unclipped plant would achieve), and cutting back hard at the usual pruning time—you want to encourage bushiness from the beginning. Don't be in too much of a hurry to get your hedge up to full height; it will be bushier and more solid if you trim the sides as it grows. Don't try to make it too narrow, either—a width of about a third of the intended height is usually about right. The hedge will be bushier if you taper it so that the bottom is about 20 per cent wider than the top. This will let the light to all the branches. Try to cut it quite vertical, and inevitably the bottom will get starved of light and grow patchy. It's well worth marking a pole (the handle of a rake is often useful) with paint or electrician's tape to give yourself a measuring rod to check height and width while you clip.

'Laying' a hedge is a skill more used in traditional British agriculture than in gardens. It was practised most often on hawthorn hedges and involved breaking the long branches halfway through, so that they could be bent in horizontally and woven into each other, like a giant piece of basketry. A freshly laid hedge looked a fright; it was just as well the job needed doing only every few years.

TOPIARY

Topiary is the shearing of individual plants into frankly artificial shapes. It has a long tradition although it goes in and out of fashion. It is not for everyone but some gardeners love it. Geometrical shapes such as cones or balls are the simplest, but with care and patience you can have peacocks, giraffes, tigers, dinosaurs, even people. It does require an appropriate setting, and it takes time and patience— but for a conversation piece a green hound chasing a row of green ducks across the lawn (as seen in one old English garden) would certainly take a lot of beating!

It's not in fact much more difficult than growing a clipped hedge, although for starters I would confine my efforts to something simple, like a cone or pyramid, or a standard with a

perfectly spherical top. Yew and box are time-honoured choices, but you could use a small-leaved privet or even one of the hybrid grevilleas such as 'Poorinda Queen'. (Be wary of plants that won't grow if cut into bare wood—you might some day need to cut hard to correct a mistake you have made.)

Start your plant, and pinch it for bushiness, as though it was going to be part of a hedge. It helps to have a framework of stakes to outline your design. A teepee would suit for a cone, but for a more complex shape such as a peacock, you may want to nail together a rough guide to tie your branches to—a bunch of growth for the head, another for the tail. And if the shape is in two parts, for instance a peacock sitting on a pedestal, use two plants, one for the pedestal and one, to be led and staked taller, for the top. Beyond that, patience and a steady hand will give you the result, eventually.

For a faster result, try moulding your shape in small-mesh chicken wire, supporting it with stakes if needed. Line the form with sphagnum moss and fill it with open, lightweight potting mix, like a hanging basket. Then plant sprigs of one of the fine-leaved ivies or the small creeping fig all over it. They will soon cover the wire and can then be clipped as needed. The 'topiary' will need as much watering and fertilising as a hanging basket, and will be happiest in the shade.

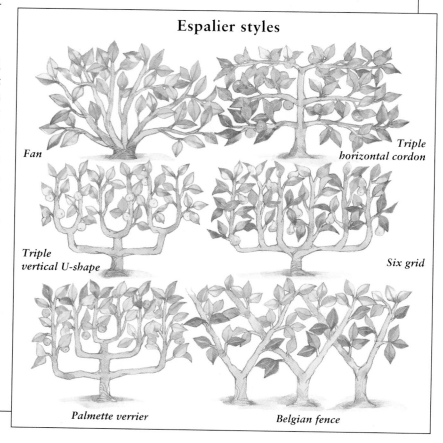

Espalier styles

Fan

Triple horizontal cordon

Triple vertical U-shape

Six grid

Palmette verrier

Belgian fence

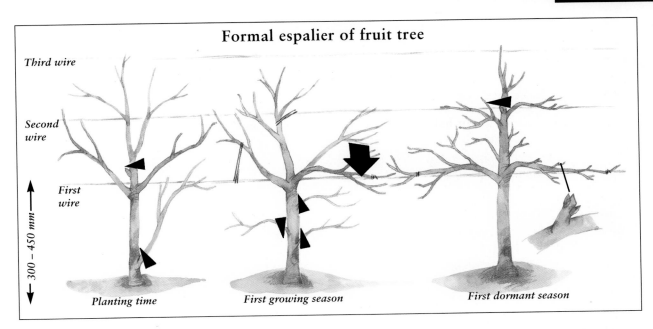

Formal espalier of fruit tree

Third wire

Second wire

First wire

300 – 450 mm

Planting time   *First growing season*   *First dormant season*

ESPALIER

The idea of training a shrub or small tree flat against a wall apparently first occurred to the ancient Romans. The idea was that a fruit tree so trained would gain reflected warmth from the wall and so its fruit would ripen earlier. Fruit trees are still classic espalier subjects and the various formal patterns in which they are traditionally trained are designed for maximum cropping. However, any plant that can take regular discipline can be espaliered and it is not obligatory to train its branches to grow in geometrical arrangements. Vines are more common wall covers but an espalier gives a more tailored effect, and as shrubs are slower growing than most climbers, it may be less work to trim an espalier once or twice a year than to be constantly curtailing a vine.

The process of training is simple enough: you plant your chosen shrub or tree against the wall, tying in the main branches that will form the basis of the desired pattern and cutting out any that are growing away from the wall. (You need a trellis, or at least some wires fixed to the wall, to which you can tie the plant.) In future years, you simply continue the process, pruning at the usual time.

POLLARDING

This is a method of pruning trees much practised in France. You cut the main branches short and allow the resulting shoots to grow for only a year or two before cutting them back very short. This controls the size of the tree to a nicety, which is why municipal engineers love treating street trees in this way, but the main point is that the many slender, leafy branches give a much denser shade than an unpollarded tree would. In time, the ends of the pruned branches develop great knobs of wood—the consolidated bases of the annual shoots—which you can find picturesque or horrible according to taste. One

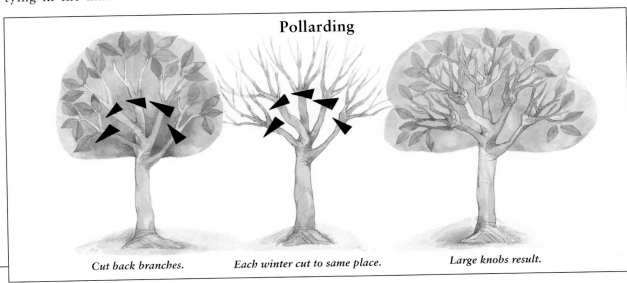

Pollarding

Cut back branches.   *Each winter cut to same place.*   *Large knobs result.*

pollarded tree on its own can certainly look tortured, but an avenue or group can look pleasingly formal in the right surroundings.

If you like the idea of pollarding, train your young tree to a tall, single stem, ensuring that the main branches are evenly spaced but otherwise leaving them to grow until they are about as thick as your wrist. Then you cut them back in winter to about 50 cm long, and head back the leader to create an even dome of foliage. The following winter (and each winter afterwards) you cut back the previous summer's growth hard, to within a few centimetres of the base. The most suitable trees are planes, celtis and catalpas. The technique is also practised on such large shrubs as crepe myrtles and poinsettias, with the aim of forcing them to produce huge clusters of flowers.

PLEACHING

Pleaching is sometimes confused with pollarding, but it is more like espaliering. You plant the chosen trees in a row and train the branches to a flat plane, interlacing them together when the trees meet, and cutting away any that threaten to grow away from the wall of foliage thus formed. (A few wires, strung between tall stakes or poles, are a great help in the early stages.) The effect is like a hedge on stilts, and when the trees have grown together to the height you want, you can clip them like a regular hedge. This is an extreme example of pruning for an artificial shape and calls for a very formal style of garden if it is not to look silly.

PRUNING TOOLS

IT IS POSSIBLE TO BUY ALL SORTS OF TOOLS for pruning, but most gardeners can get by with two: a pair of secateurs and a pruning saw. You might also add a long-handled pair of loppers, which are simply secateurs with long handles for applying extra force. They are valuable for those in-between sized branches that are a bit too big for the secateurs but not quite big enough to really need a saw, and for reaching up into trees. You might also find long-handled pruning saws useful. Hedge shears are only of use if you have a hedge or topiary to shear; they aren't any use for cutting woody stems. Unless you have a lot of hedges to trim, electric shears are an extravagance; if you do buy them, remember that they are only useful for soft growth, and buy a rechargeable model rather than one that will have you trailing many metres of flex around the garden. Not only is that an inconvenience, you run the risk of cutting live flex and shocking yourself into hospital or worse. Old-fashioned gardeners swear by the trusty pruning knife, but it needs a skilled, leather-tough hand; most of us will opt for secateurs. Nonetheless, a razor-sharp knife is useful for cleaning up saw cuts that might be a bit ragged. Any stout kitchen knife can be pressed into service if the cook will let it out in the garden; I like to use a small paring knife.

Pleaching

Plant young trees at foot of wires.

As they grow, tie branches to wires and cut off any growing forward.

Positioning pruning shears

Right   Wrong

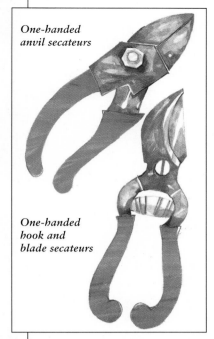

One-handed anvil secateurs

One-handed hook and blade secateurs

Why you should never leave a stump! There is a real danger of rot spreading into the trunk.

Secateurs come in two types: the more common (and better) has a cutting blade that passes a hook which grabs the branch, the other cuts against an anvil. The anvil type is a little cheaper, but it tends to crush the stem as you cut, which is not good. Whichever one you choose, it is worth buying the best quality you can afford. Buy them full-size; if they are well-balanced, they won't be tiring to use. Try them in your hand before you buy. (Left-handed models are available, too, although you may have to search for them.) The small models (which used to be called 'ladies models') are really only useful for cutting flowers. Serious pruning work is beyond their scope. Secateurs should be given a drop of oil occasionally. They should be sharp enough to cut stiff paper, but they are not easy to sharpen and so they should be disassembled first. (I still have a pair that I couldn't for the life of me get back together again; their successors go to a professional knife sharpener once a year.) The same considerations apply to loppers. Buy the best and keep them sharp. Whether they have wooden or metal handles is a matter of taste.

The most useful kind of saw is the one with a tapering, curved blade, which can get into tight corners with ease. Its teeth will be coarser than a carpenter's saw, but if they are sharp they will cut pretty cleanly, and you can always trim the cut with a knife if you think it a bit ragged. Folding saws, where the blade folds away into a groove in the handle, are safer in storage, although they are apt to be a bit light for pruning trees, and if the saw decides to fold itself up while you are using it the consequences can be messy and painful. Bigger hand saws with still coarser teeth are useful for big limbs, and you can buy pruning saws with coarse teeth on one side, fine on the other. The idea is better in theory than in practice; in a tight corner you can find the back of the saw cutting a branch you want to keep. You can also buy the ordinary curved saw with a long handle, which is useful for extending your reach. It isn't quite as easy to control as the usual short-handled variety, and a bit of practice on branches you are planning to cut off lower down is desirable. If you are faced with limbs large enough to call for a chain saw you are probably at the stage when professional help is needed; chain saws are dangerous in unfamiliar hands. Sharpening a saw is a job for a professional, and you may find it cheaper, with the basic curved saw at any rate, to buy a cheap new one. They aren't very expensive.

Hedge shears are really just enormous scissors. There isn't much to choose in the various models, although here I should opt for the lightest. The standard blade is about 20 cm long; longer blades are useful if you have a lot of shearing to do, but they are heavier and if you tire under the weight your ability to clip precisely will suffer. Long-handled models are available and would be worth considering if you have tall hedges to prune; they save either stretching overhead or climbing on a stepladder. You will still need a regular pair, however, for the top of the hedge, and the long handles are cumbersome in use. If I had a big hedge, I would buy electric hedge trimmers, but delicate work on corners or fancy topiary is more precise with hand shears.

A ladder is useful to have; you can't cut precisely if you are reaching up on tiptoe. Aluminium ladders are long lasting and light, although a heavier, wooden ladder is apt to be more stable. Be very careful with a stepladder; it needs firm footing to be stable. When you get up on a ladder, it really is best to have a second person to hold it steady.

CARING FOR TOOLS

Cutting through wood dulls tools quite quickly and sap congeals on them. Wipe them clean with a damp rag (methylated spirits or turpentine will remove any stubborn deposits and won't help rust start) and wipe them over with an oily rag from time to time. Unless you are very skilled with the whetstone, it is best to send them to a professional sharpener. A good hardware store should be able to put you in touch with one.

PLANTING

It has never been easier to buy plants. Every suburb and small town these days seems to have its garden centre; supermarkets and big chain stores have garden departments, even if all they offer are seeds and packets of bulbs; many florists sell pot plants and seedlings as well as cut flowers; and the gardening magazines are filled with advertisements from growers wanting to send plants to you by post. So why go to the trouble of propagating your own?

Named varieties of rhododendron are propagated vegetatively, by layering or grafting. You would only grow them from seed if you were hoping to create new varieties.

MOST OBVIOUSLY, FOR ECONOMY. PLANTS aren't really very expensive, not when you consider the nursery has to meet expenses and still make a profit, but to buy all you need to furnish a garden can add up to a lot of money. Buy just a few and multiply them yourself and you come out ahead. Then again, a friend may have a desirable plant that the local nursery does not. Take a cutting, or save some seeds, and you have it too; and with it the happy memories that accompany any gift. Perhaps you just take a particular liking to a plant and want to have more of it, or a favourite is coming to the end of its life, or perhaps you are planning to move house and want to take your favourite plants with you. Then there's the sheer fun of propagating; raising plants from infancy is one of the most satisfying things in gardening.

The equipment you need for propagating is simple, and you will already have most of the necessary tools: secateurs, a rake, a spade, a trowel or a fork. A single-sided razor blade will do duty for trimming cuttings and can be pressed into service for budding and grafting too, although if you do a lot of these you may want to search out a specialised grafting knife. Warmth is a great help propagating both seeds

Lettuce is an annual, and therefore must be grown from seed. Plant breeders try to ensure that the seedlings of their named strains are as uniform as possible.

and cuttings—a greenhouse will greatly increase your success but a cold frame will do just as well. You could make a cold frame from an old window and some treated pine—it is essentially just a wide box with a glass lid—or even improvise a mini-frame from an old broccoli box and some plastic wrap. Set your frame in a lightly shaded position so you warm your baby plants but don't cook them in the hot sun!

WAYS OF PROPAGATING

ANIMALS CAN BE REPRODUCED ONLY BY means of sex, but plants offer the gardener the choice of being increased either sexually, that is by seed, or asexually (English speakers, unlike the French, usually prefer the less emotive term vegetatively) from single individuals by such means as cuttings, layering, division or by grafting.

Seedlings combine the genes of two parents, and the chances are that they will be subtly or markedly different from either. (Nurseries have to take care to keep the strains of plants that are regularly propagated from seed, such as annuals and most vegetables, pure so that variation will be minimal.) Vegetative propagation, on the other hand, ensures that the new plant will be a replica of its sole parent, and there will be no surprises. A group of plants so propagated from a single individual is known as a clone, and most named varieties of garden plants are clones, the reproduced progeny of outstanding individuals selected from many, many seedlings. Sow the seed of one of

these—a 'Granny Smith' apple, a 'Peace' rose, a 'Fuerte' avocado—and the seedlings will not only be unlike their parent, the chances are they will be inferior. But remember that the new plant will carry any viruses with which its parent may be afflicted, and select your propagating material only from healthy plants.

GROWING PLANTS FROM SEED

SOME PEOPLE ARE RATHER NERVOUS about growing plants from seed, and while it is true that infant seedlings need devoted care, there are compensating advantages. Annuals, which include most vegetables, can only be grown from seed, and though you can buy seedlings you limit yourself to only the most popular varieties. Growing a rare plant from seed is often the easiest way of acquiring it. (But if you plan to buy seeds from overseas, do check with the Department of Agriculture that you are allowed to import them.) Very few plant diseases are transmitted through the seed, and so seedlings start life with a clean bill of health. If, for instance, you have a favourite lily, which is succumbing to virus, you can save some seed and so rescue your stock. Finally, there are some plants that are much more easily propagated from seed than vegetatively, acacias and eucalypts being the outstanding examples.

Growing seeds is simple enough in principle. You sow them in fine textured soil, covering them to a depth equal to the size of the seed, and water them gently until they come up. When the baby plants are big enough to handle, they are transplanted ('pricked out') into another

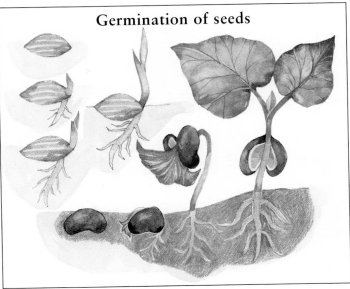

Germination of seeds

Planting seedlings

1 Seedlings often come in punnets of six. If they come in plastic pots like egg cartons, cut them up individually.

2 The easiest way to get the seedlings out is to tip the punnet upside down, holding plants between fingers.

pot or bed to give them more room so that they can become big enough to plant out in their final growing positions.

SOWING SEEDS OUTDOORS

There are various refinements on the process. Many seeds can be sown direct where they are to spend all their lives, and the gardener then thins the seedlings to the strongest and best spaced. Nasturtiums, sweet peas and most vegetables are treated this way. The important thing is to have the bed cultivated to a fine tilth so that the soil won't cake over the emerging seedlings and to water gently. Put out snail bait, so that you won't lose your seedlings as soon as they come up. It's easiest to sow in rows, making a furrow of the appropriate depth with a pointed stick. Big seeds such as nasturtiums or pumpkins can be sown at their final spacings (you might like to put two or three at each station and remove all but the strongest seedling if all come up), but smaller seeds are dribbled in along the furrow. It helps to get an even distribution if you bulk them up with dry sand.

You can prepare a nursery bed in a convenient, lightly shaded place, out of the way of children and romping pets. Adding some sand to the soil will help its texture. If you think there might be weed seeds, water the bed well to encourage them to germinate, zap them with glyphosate, and wait two weeks for the chemical to disperse before sowing. Then you make your furrows, about 3 cm apart, and sow your seeds as before. Small seeds can easily be buried too deep—just sprinkle a very little fine soil over them. Water very gently, with the finest spray the hose or watering can gives, and keep the soil evenly moist until the seedlings have come up: the last thing you want is for them to dry out. An old trick is to lay a piece of hessian over the seed bed. This both conserves moisture and breaks the force of the hose, but you must remove it as soon as you see signs of emerging seedlings. Start lifting a corner of the hessian after a week or so to check.

SOWING SEEDS IN CONTAINERS

THE GREAT ADVANTAGE OF SOWING SEEDS in containers is that it gives you complete control of their growing conditions. This is especially an advantage with spring sown seed, when cold snaps may be a problem: you can sow in the greenhouse if you have one, or on a sunny

Some extra warmth helps the germination of seeds and the striking of cuttings. Here is an economical alternative to the wood-and-glass propagating frame—simply a sheet of kitchen wrap stretched over the top of a polystyrene box.

window sill indoors, and have them ready for transplanting earlier than you would if they were grown outside. It's much easier to handle small seeds and tiny seedlings in a container at bench height than down on your knees, and you can give each container its own individual attention. By all means sow seeds in regular flower pots, but the ideal container is wider and shallower—you need area rather than depth of soil, except for tree seeds where depth is important. The old-fashioned wooden seed tray, about 30 cm square and 6 cm deep, is easy enough to knock together, but ingenuity will suggest alternatives. You might try egg cartons, flat plastic take-away food boxes or even the waxed paper trays greengrocers use to display soft fruit. Just make some holes in the bottom for drainage.

Fill your containers with fine potting soil. The finest and crumbliest compost from the compost heap mixed with sand (about two parts of compost to one of sand) should do fine, or you can buy specially formulated seed sowing mixes ready made. Both container and soil should be sterile to guard against the damping-off fungus, the chief cause of disaster with small seedlings. Used flower pots can be swabbed out with bleach and allowed to dry, and the soil mix can be put in the microwave oven for a couple of minutes. Let it cool down before sowing!

Sow your seeds as usual. You can enclose small containers in a plastic bag, or spread plastic food wrap across the top of a bigger one to keep everything warm and moist, but uncover your containers as soon as germination is under way—fresh air is a great preventative of damping off. (If it does strike, and you find seedlings collapsing and rotting, spray the container with a fungicide at once.)

The time needed for germination varies very much. Most annuals and vegetables will appear in ten days to a fortnight or so, with some taking three weeks, but shrubs and trees may take much longer. Some trees, sown in autumn, need exposure to winter cold before germinating in the spring. Don't be in too much haste to throw out a container of seeds that hasn't come up yet! Some seeds (especially among the legumes, the pea family) have a hard casing that has to be softened before they can germinate. The simplest way of doing this is to soak them in warm water for a couple of hours and then sow them at once; the encyclopaedia entries draw your attention to them.

All being well, your seeds will germinate in such abundance that they will be crowded if you leave them long in the sowing container or bed. Once they start to make their true leaves, they are ready to be pricked out. You need to be very gentle—lift them with a small pointed stick or a fine screwdriver (I got into trouble as a child for using a silver cake fork), and either relocate them to a new container or a fresh part of the nursery bed, setting them about 5 cm apart. Water them in, and give them some shade for a few days—a newspaper tent is fine. When they have settled in, they can be given some slow-release fertiliser, and once they have made three or four sets of leaves they are ready to go in their final positions. You may want to pot up trees, shrubs or perennials, giving them royal treatment for a few months or a year until they are big enough for the garden.

ACQUIRING SEEDS

The simplest way to acquire seeds is to buy them, and seeds grown and packaged by a reliable seed company should give you every success if you follow the directions on the packet. Don't forget that seeds are not immortal—sow before the 'sow by' date. You can save extra seeds for a later sowing (for example, you may want to make successive sowings of vegetables to ensure a longer crop), but don't try to save them for next year. Seed is not all that expensive, and stale seed rarely germinates satisfactorily.

SAVING YOUR OWN SEEDS

You can, of course, save seed from your own plants, and it is easy to do. Let the seeds ripen on the plant, gathering them before they are shed. Plants with fleshy fruit, such as tomatoes, are easy: pick the fruit when ripe, remove the flesh and dry the seeds before storing them. Those that ripen to dryness and then shed are a trifle more tricky—you want to pick the ripening seed just before it departs the plant. As soon as the seeds look as though they are about to be shed, tie a paper or muslin bag over

When these clematis seeds have ripened to fluffy dryness, they will come away easily in your hand. Don't worry if a few blow away—you won't need them all.

the developing seed heads, and let them fall into that. Once seed is being released, you can pick the heads, paper bag and all, and hang them up in the shed to finish drying out. Often you can just gather the seeds in your hand. When the seeds are quite dry, you can funnel them into a small sealed container (the plastic jars that pills come in are as good as any), label and date them, and then store them in the fridge. The dry cold will keep them fresh until it is time for you to sow them.

Some plants so interbreed in gardens that the seedlings won't 'come true', aquilegias and grevilleas being notorious examples, although they may well give you some pleasant surprises. But beware of taking seed from what are known as F1 and F2 hybrids. Many vegetable varieties are hybrids these days, and so are some of the best varieties of such flowers as petunias and marigolds. These are the result of crossing two carefully selected parent strains, and the cross has to be made afresh every time a crop of seed is wanted.

HYBRIDISING

You can gather seeds just as the plant produces them, but it can be fun to cross-pollinate your flowers to see whether you can come up with anything new and different. You might like to try your hand with bearded irises, gladioli or daylilies, all of which have fairly large and easily manipulated matrimonial parts and easily grow from seed. Roses are trickier, as they aren't very easy to grow from seed, and seedling camellias take ages to bloom, but if they are your favourites, go ahead! Many a fine variety has been 'raised' by an amateur hybridist.

The principle is the same for all flowers. First choose your parents for the combination of characters you would like to see—you might, for instance, want to combine the ruffled petals of a pink gladiolus with the deep colour of a red one. Before the flower which is to be mother has quite opened, remove its stamens so that it won't pollinate itself (stripping the petals can make the plant easier to handle) and cover it with a small paper bag in case of wandering bees. Then, when the flower is (or would be) fully open, brush the stigma with a pollen bearing stamen from your chosen father. (Detach it and carry it with tweezers if necessary.) Put the paper bag back in the interests of chastity, until the flower withers and fertilisation is no longer possible. All having gone according to plan, the seeds can be gathered when ripe and sown at the

Pollinating bearded irises

Remove the pollen-covered anther from one plant and wipe it on the outer edge of the stigma of another.

appropriate time, and in due course you will have a collection of new, unique flowers of your own. Maybe one will be sufficiently distinctive and beautiful to name in honour of your mother, the cat, or even yourself! But a word of caution: if you are making several crosses, label everything at all stages or you'll forget which seedlings came from which cross.

VEGETATIVE PROPAGATION

VEGETATIVE PROPAGATION IS DONE IN one of three basic ways: by removing a part of the plant that already has roots (by dividing a clump of perennials or bulbs), by removing a part that hasn't roots and inducing it to make roots (by taking a cutting or making a layer) or by uniting a rootless piece to one that is already rooted and growing (by one of the several forms of grafting). Let us look at them in turn.

DIVISION

Division is probably the simplest means of propagating—a plant multiplies itself into a clump, and you simply lift it from the ground, separate it into several sections and replant them. It is easiest if the clump just falls to pieces when you shake the soil from its roots, but often you have to apply that combination of force and

Like many perennials, peonies make tightly bound clumps, and you may need a sharp knife to cut them apart.

Layering

Stake to hold plant steady

Shoot stripped of leaves and buried

gentleness that so much of gardening (not the least pruning) demands. The classic method is to thrust two forks back to back into the centre of the clump, but who has two forks these days? The solution here is to cut the clump apart with secateurs or a sharp knife, which won't come to much harm if you clean them promptly. The best propagations are almost always the young, strong growths from the outside of the clump. Don't try to break up the clump into smaller divisions than come fairly easily.

Division is most appropriate with perennials and bulbs, but some thicket-forming shrubs such as snowberries *(Symphoricarpos)*, ceratostigma and some shrub roses can be divided too, or you can detach rooted suckers, which go by the delightful name of Irishman's cuttings.

LAYERING
Many trailing plants layer themselves, forming roots where their shoots or runners touch the ground—examples are ivy grown as a ground-cover, strawberries, ajuga—and these can be simply detached and replanted. Blackberries and their relatives will root spontaneously where a branch bends to touch the ground (one of the ways in which feral blackberries make such nuisances of themselves) and most shrubs that can be bent low enough can be induced to do the same. The procedure is simple enough—bend a suitable branch down, make a nick at the lowest point, bury it, and when it has made roots in a few weeks or months, detach the new plant and transplant it. You need to hold the branch still, either by putting a brick on top of the buried

section or, better, by staking the far end of your branch. Layering is particularly valuable with plants such as rhododendrons that root only slowly from cuttings. But any plant that will grow from cuttings can be layered, and if you only want a couple of plants it is a less trouble-some way to get them—you just set and forget for a few weeks. Just make sure you don't accidentally dig up your layers when weeding.

Although not all gardeners agree, I think it is worth brushing rooting hormone onto the nick when layering and air-layering. Use a liquid version of any of the available brands, but take care to ensure it is fresh as rooting hormone loses its potency quickly.

AIR-LAYERING
What if you can't bend a branch down to the ground? You take the soil to the plant, in what is called air-layering or marcottage. Select the point where you want roots to grow, make a nick in the stem there (tie it above and below to a cane if you fear it will break) and pack some

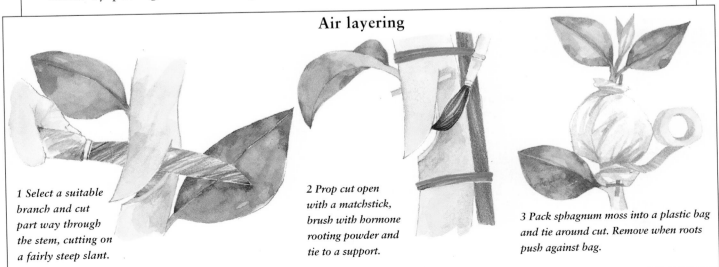

Air layering

1 Select a suitable branch and cut part way through the stem, cutting on a fairly steep slant.

2 Prop cut open with a matchstick, brush with hormone rooting powder and tie to a support.

3 Pack sphagnum moss into a plastic bag and tie around cut. Remove when roots push against bag.

wet sphagnum moss or peat moss around it, tying all in place with a piece of polythene. When you see roots through the plastic, cut the whole thing off and plant it (taking the plastic away, of course.) Air-layering is the traditional way of cutting the too-tall office rubber tree to size—air layer the top metre or so, and give the new plant the old one's pot—but it can be done to almost any shrub that will strike roots from a layering or cutting. The only thing to watch is that the moss doesn't dry out.

Cuttings

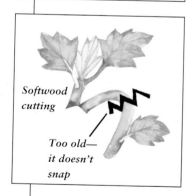

Nodal cutting with cut below node or joint

Heel cutting with old wood at base

Softwood cutting

Too old— it doesn't snap

Root growth is increased with auxin and Vitamin B added to the soil.

CUTTINGS

Cuttings are the next stage—you remove a part of the plant that has no roots and place it in soil in such conditions that it will be kept alive until roots develop and it can start to support itself. Normally, you take a piece of the stem, either one that is actively growing (softwood or tip cuttings), one that has stopped growing but is not quite mature (half-ripe or semi-mature cuttings) or one that is quite mature and firm (it may indeed have gone into dormancy and lost its leaves—mature or hardwood cuttings).

Whatever type of cutting you use, there are a couple of things to watch. Most plants make roots best from a node in the stem, the point from which a leaf arises, and that is where you cut. Make sure you haven't bruised anything and that the cut is perfectly clean—cut the stem longer than needed and trim it down with a razor blade if need be. Remove all leaves that will be buried. You can cut the remaining leaves in half to reduce moisture loss if you like. With the best of care, a 100 per cent strike is unusual—always take a few more cuttings than you think you'll need. If you have a choice, take your cuttings from young, more vigorous plants rather than from old, sedate ones, or at least from vigorous shoots—and always, from the choicest, healthiest plants you have.

The process of rooting is interesting to follow—first the cut surfaces heal over with a white callus and then the roots sprout from the callus. How long this takes varies with the species. Be patient—as

A well-rooted coleus cutting being transplanted to its own pot. It is only about a month since it was taken.

long as your cutting hasn't died, the process is underway. There is no harm in tipping the cuttings out of their pot to check after a few weeks, but don't disturb them. Opinions differ as to whether it is worth dipping cuttings in rooting hormone. Some people think it makes little difference, but I think it really does help. Use any of the available brands, although liquid hormones are preferable to powder formulas—but make sure it is fresh. It loses its potency rather quickly, and an old bottle will be useless.

Hardwood cuttings can be struck outside, by setting them in the same sort of bed in which you would grow seeds, but soft and half-ripe cuttings need some protection. The simplest way is to put them up in pots of very sandy soil (three parts of sharp sand to one of regular potting mix is fine), and enclose each pot in a plastic bag to keep everything moist and humid. The technology-minded might like to investigate a 'mist propagation' system, which keeps the cuttings bathed in a constant, controlled fog. This allows even recalcitrant plants such as rhododendrons to be grown from cuttings, but the equipment is elaborate and expensive.

ROOT CUTTINGS

Cuttings are normally made from pieces of stem, but you can also take root cuttings of many plants. Just dig up a nice fat root, cut it into

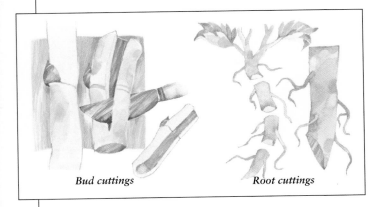

Bud cuttings　　　　　*Root cuttings*

sections about 10 cm long, and put them in a pot. If you can't remember which way was up, lay them horizontally. Root cuttings are the best way to propagate acanthus, the princess tree (*Paulownia tomentosa*) and wisteria, but try them with peonies, perennial phlox and *Romneya coulteri*.

LEAF CUTTINGS

Leaf cuttings are more esoteric—they are really only used with African violets and their relatives, and with begonias. You just snip off a leaf and treat it like any other cutting.

A TECHNIQUE YOU PROBABLY CAN'T USE

Even more esoteric is mericlonal propagation, where a few cells are taken from the very end of the growing tip of a shoot and cultured on a sterile medium. They develop a great mass of callus, which can be cut into sections and, by varying the nutrient medium, made to develop into plants. If this sounds like a laboratory technique, you are quite right. However, it has proved useful in propagating kangaroo paws, and in creating great numbers of plants of such things as daffodils and orchids very quickly and more cheaply than by waiting for the slow process of natural division. At the very end of the shoot, the cells are dividing so fast that viruses can't catch up with them, and so clean plants can be created from virus-infected stock.

GRAFTING

Grafting is the union of one plant (the scion) with the roots of another (the stock or understock). Although it is one of the oldest of the gardener's arts, there is no need for most of us to master it—seed, cuttings, layering and division should serve for just about everything. So when would you go to the trouble of grafting? Perhaps you have a camellia that is too established and flourishing to discard but has flowers that don't appeal to you—you can convert it to a plant you like by grafting, or you could even try grafting several different varieties on it to create a multi-coloured tree. Or you could change the variety on a grape vine, something wine growers do when fashionable varieties change. Most often, however, grafting is used to control the growth of the scion, either by giving it the benefit of more vigorous roots than it would make for itself (as when roses are budded on wild rose roots) or, conversely, by using a less vigorous, 'dwarfing' stock, a technique used especially with apples and pears to create smaller, more manageable trees. The benefits of doing this are such that roses and fruit trees are almost all grafted, but the possibilities are limited for those of us not in the nursery trade by the difficulty of obtaining the strains used for understocks. (This is a matter of supply and demand: backyard gardeners rarely want to buy understock varieties.)

Although grafting isn't difficult, it does call for a certain amount of care. What you are

Budding (or shield grafting)

1 Cut the bud from the stem with a sliver of bark. Don't let it dry out.

2 Make a shallow T-cut in bark of understock and lift flaps. If bark is stiff, water heavily and wait a day or two.

3 Slip bud behind flaps and bind with raffia or budding tape.

When the petals fall, the buds on a rose stem will be ready for propagating—but don't try to use any that are sprouting and select only from strong, healthy branches.

doing is making a wound on the stock plant and inserting a piece of scion (a cutting, if you like) into it, in the hope that both stock and scion will callus together and make the union. This means that you must match the cambium layers, the green section of stem immediately below the bark, together perfectly, for that is where the callus arises. This calls for razor-sharp blades to make the cuts, and a steady hand to make the match precisely!

The simplest form of grafting is budding (or shield grafting), which is the method most often used for roses and fruit trees. Shakespeare described it aptly as 'the insertion beneath the baser bark of a bud of nobler race'—you lift a flap of bark on the understock (which has been grown from seed or a cutting), and slip in a growth bud from the scion, trimmed to give just a sliver of bark to support it. Cambium matching is automatic, and you bind everything together with raffia or plastic tape. Pictures show the process easier than words. It is important to have the stock growing furiously, with the sap running freely, and the bud at just the right stage of maturity, no longer young but not yet quite mature. Some time around mid-summer usually sees everything at the right stage. After budding, you let the stock grow, cutting it off just above the bud the following winter. Come spring, the bud will grow away to start the branches of your new plant.

Cleft grafting is the other important method. With it you cut off the stock first, cleave it with a sharp knife and insert your scion in the cleft (or two, one on either side), matching the cambiums with exquisite precision. All the wounded surfaces are then covered with grafting wax and, if you like, you can enclose the graft with a plastic bag to keep the scion from drying out. The best time for this is towards the end of dormancy, when the sap has begun to run but not so much that the stock will bleed to death when you behead it. The understock can be a young plant or mature branch, which will need several grafts.

Other forms of grafting, such as approach grafting, whip-and-tongue grafting, veneer grafting and their like, are best left to the professionals.

Splice grafting

Scion and stock showing long slanting cuts

In position and tied with raffia or plastic tape

Cleft grafting

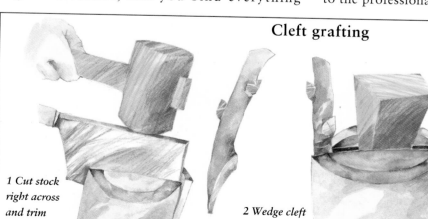

1 Cut stock right across and trim scions to a long wedge to fit.

2 Wedge cleft open. Insert scions on either side of cleft, matching green cambium layers exactly.

3 Remove wedge and bind tightly with raffia or plastic tape. Coat with grafting wax.

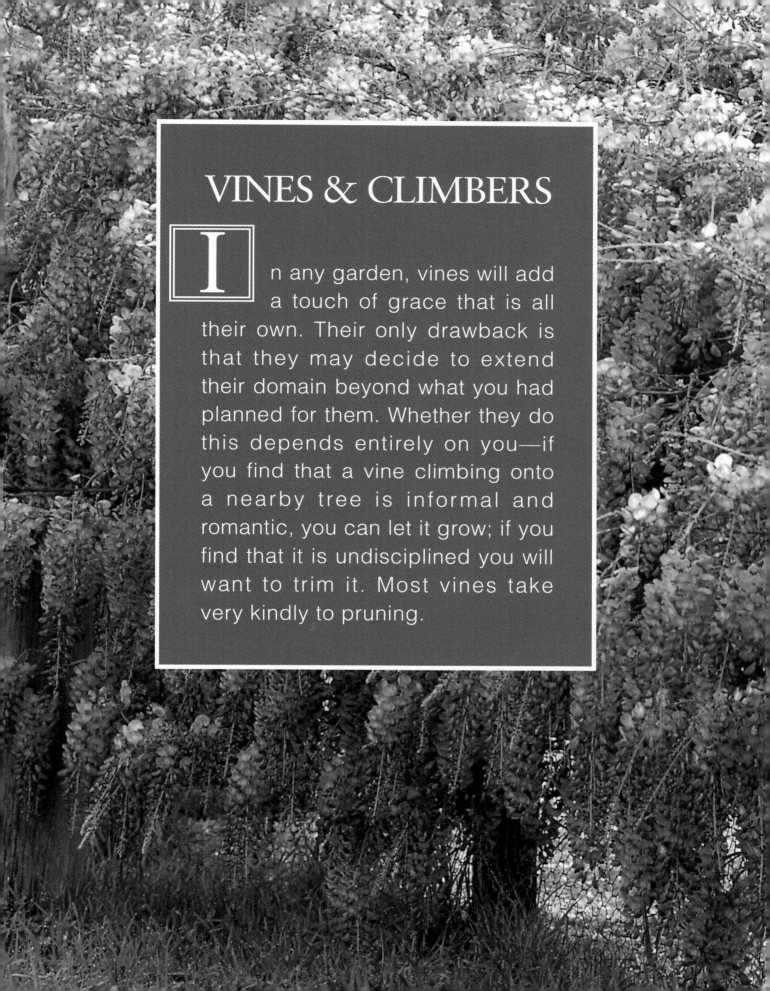

VINES & CLIMBERS

In any garden, vines will add a touch of grace that is all their own. Their only drawback is that they may decide to extend their domain beyond what you had planned for them. Whether they do this depends entirely on you—if you find that a vine climbing onto a nearby tree is informal and romantic, you can let it grow; if you find that it is undisciplined you will want to trim it. Most vines take very kindly to pruning.

ALLAMANDA
Allamanda
Evergreen vines, flowering from late spring to autumn.

A. cathartica is a strong climber, needing the usual training and shortening of out-of-bounds shoots; it can be headed back and thinned out in early spring to control its size. With regular heading back after each flush of bloom it can be used as a tub plant. *A. neriifolia* is more of a shrub, and with heading back as needed can be kept quite compact. Occasionally remove a couple of the oldest stems after bloom. In cool areas, wait until the weather has warmed up before you start to do any pruning.
Propagation Easy, by layering or you can take half-ripe cuttings in summer.

BLEEDING HEART VINE
Clerodendrum thomsoniae
Evergreen shrubby vine, flowering in summer.

Although not strictly a climber, this makes an excellent informal espalier. It benefits from thinning out of some of the oldest wood and heading back long branches in early spring; you can also trim after bloom for neatness.
Propagation Quite easy, from half-ripe cuttings in summer.

BLUEBELL CREEPER
Sollya heterophylla
Fast growing, evergreen vine, flowering in spring and summer.

You can grow this West Australian native in three ways: as a climber, a shrub or a groundcover. As a climber it needs a trellis. Train the young shoots horizontally at first or it will grow straight up and get bare at the base; when it is established, pinch wayward young shoots or give the plant a light trim in early spring. Or it will form a compact shrub if allowed to twine over itself. Give it no support, but pinch the young plant to make it bushy and regularly head back any shoots that grow away from the main outline. As a groundcover it needs no support but disentangle any stems twining about each other to allow the young plants to lie flat. All you need to do thereafter is trim back any shoots that threaten to grow upright instead of along the ground.
Propagation Easy, by layering or cuttings (either softwood or half-ripe) in summer or by spring-sown seed.

BOUGAINVILLEA
Bougainvillea
Rapid growing, woody vines, evergreen or deciduous according to climate, flowering several times a year.

You can leave a bougainvillea unpruned, but it might take over the garden. Fortunately, they can be kept at almost any size you want by regular pruning. The best time is after flowering, when the shoots that have just flowered should be headed back and long branches shortened to within bounds. Strong young shoots can be pinched back several times as they grow; this will curtail their length and the short side shoots that pinching encourages will bear more flowers. If a strong shoot threatens to grow in an unwanted direction, remove it altogether. If the plants are pruned after every cycle of bloom, they shouldn't need hard pruning to keep them in bounds. Don't overwater and fertilise, which encourages growth at the expense of flowers; the plants grow wild in climates where cycles of drought are followed by rain and flowers. You can prune a plant that is too big quite savagely; it will respond with massive new growth, which should be pinched and disciplined as it develops. The plant will probably miss a flowering or two, but blooms will appear once growth slows down. Don't fertilise during this time of growth until the plant is flowering again.
Propagation Easy, by layering in summer.

CAPE HONEYSUCKLE
Tecomaria capensis
Evergreen, shrubby vine, flowering in early summer.

The cape honeysuckle can be trained to a trellis like any other vine, when it will need only routine training, thinning and heading back if it gets out of bounds; but you can also, by regular pinching and trimming, grow it as a shrub or even as a hedge. The best pruning time is in early spring. Hedges should be trimmed, with secateurs rather than shears, after each batch of flowers is over.
Propagation Easy, by layering or by half-ripe cuttings taken at any time from early spring to early autumn.

CAROLINA JASMINE
Gelsemium sempervirens
Evergreen vine, flowering in late winter and spring.

A slender twiner, the Carolina jasmine needs only an occasional thinning out of tangled or crowded growth, a job best done after flowering. It can, however, take quite hard pruning if it has got out of hand. It makes a pleasing groundcover, needing only the cutting back of over-tall stems at any time.
Propagation Easy, by layering or by taking half-ripe cuttings in summer.

Trained on a pergola, bougainvillea needs regular thinning or after a few years all you will see from below is a great heap of branches. Mind the sharp thorns.

CHILEAN JASMINE
Mandevilla
Evergreen twining vines, flowering in summer.

The white mandevilla, *M. laxa (suaveolens)*, is apt to make a tangle of thin shoots, and it benefits from thinning and rearranging on its support in early spring, after cold weather is over but before growth begins. The pink-flowered types such as 'Alice du Pont' and 'Red Riding Hood' are shrubbier and more restrained in their growth; they need much less attention after their initial training. Head over-long shoots back in early spring, and if the plant gets bare at the base cut one or two branches back hard to force growth to come lower down.

Propagation Easy, by layering or by taking half-ripe cuttings in summer.

CHINESE TRUMPET VINE
Campsis
Deciduous, self-clinging vines, flowering in summer.

These are rampant growers, running to the top of the fence or wall on which they are growing and making a top-heavy mass of tangled growth, which often comes away from the support. (The vine is more secure, and easier to train, if you give it a trellis.) In late winter, thin out excess branches, heading back those you keep to two or three buds from the main stems. To keep the plant well clothed to the base, cut one or two branches back almost to the ground, and pinch the young growth regularly. If the plant is completely out of hand, cut it right back to the ground.

Propagation Easy, by layering, detaching suckers or taking hardwood cuttings in autumn or spring.

A cape honeysuckle as overgrown as this needs to be cut right down; then it can be trained on the fence again.

This Clematis montana *'Rubens' is at Merry Garth, Mount Wilson, NSW. It is the best known of the spring-flowering group, pruned immediately after bloom.*

These spur-pruned grape vines at Beechworth, Vic., trained in the traditional manner on two supports, have been bearing lavishly for many years.

CLEMATIS
Clematis
Evergreen or deciduous vines, flowering in spring or summer.

You can allow clematis to grow in a glorious tangle or prune to keep them under control and ensure the flowers are well displayed. They fall into three main groups. The first, which includes C. *montana* and the evergreen C. *aristata* and C. *armandii*, flower in spring on growth made last summer. They are pruned immediately after bloom, ruthlessly cutting away all the wood that has just flowered, training and redirecting the remaining branches if need be. The second are those that flower in summer, on new growth of the current season. They can be pruned in winter or earliest spring, thinning out weak growth, cutting the remainder back about halfway and rearranging the plants on their supports if needed to ensure an even coverage. If you prefer, you can cut the plants back to about half a metre above the ground, so that they will renew themselves almost entirely. This group includes many (but not all) of the large flowered hybrids such as 'Jackmanii' and 'Ville de Lyon', as well as C. *florida* and the yellow C. *tangutica*. The third group, which includes many other large flowered hybrids such as 'Nellie Moser' and 'The President', flower both in late spring on last year's growth, and again in summer on new shoots. Prune these lightly in winter, just enough so that you can disentangle and arrange the stems to best advantage. Then, after bloom, cut away the shoots that have just flowered to encourage the strong new shoots that will bear the later flowers. If you are faced with a plant of uncertain pedigree, let it grow as it pleases for a couple of years until you find out to which group it belongs. If you rush in and prune before you know, you may find you have no flowers that year.

Propagation Fairly easy. Species can be grown from seed sown in autumn; hybrids are best from half-ripe cuttings or from layering in summer. Clematis are often grafted, but most of us will find it easier to take cuttings.

FALSE SARSAPARILLA
Hardenbergia
Evergreen vines, flowering during spring months.

Not usually big enough to train over pergolas, these can be trained on fences, as ground-cover or, in bush gardens, allowed to scramble over shrubs and the lower branches of trees. They need only an occasional thinning out and disentangling after flowering. Pinching young growth will help control the plant's spread and prevent it from getting bare at the base.

Propagation Easy, by layering in summer or seed in spring. Soak the seeds for a few hours before sowing and they will germinate faster.

FLAME CREEPER
Pyrostegia venusta, syn. *Bignonia venusta*
Fast growing, evergreen vine, climbing by tendrils and flowering in winter or early spring.

Left to itself, this spectacular climbing plant rapidly becomes a tangle, but the flowers come on new growth, and so it will take any amount of discipline, preferably right after bloom.

Propagation Easy, by layering or by taking half-ripe cuttings in summer.

FRUIT SALAD PLANT
Monstera deliciosa
Evergreen, slow growing climber, flowering in early summer.

Often grown as an indoor plant, this will make a very substantial vine in frost-free climates, clinging to walls and fences by its long aerial roots. Either indoors or out, it can be controlled by cutting back the stems at almost any time, but early spring is best. The fruit salad plant will sprout readily even from a bare stem. The aerial roots of plants grown indoors should be led into the soil in the pot rather than being cut off.

Propagation Very easy, by layering, air-layering or cuttings of the main stem, taken with a couple of incipient aerial roots. Any time during warm weather will be suitable for these processes.

GOLDEN CHALICE VINE
Solandra maxima, S. nitida
Fast growing, evergreen climber, flowering in late spring through late summer.

This massively rampant vine with thick, woody stems needs a strong support and shouldn't be trained through iron lace as the stems will crack it. If it is left unpruned, it will cover a vast area, but its foliage will be sparse and the flowers few. In late winter or early spring, head back over-long stems as hard as you need to keep the plant in bounds, and then follow up by pinching out the new growth. The result will be a more luxuriant-looking plant and more of the huge flowers. If a plant is really out of control, cut it back very hard in early spring and keep pinching as it grows back.

Propagation Easy, by layering or by taking half-ripe cuttings in summer.

GRAPE
Vitis vinifera
Deciduous vine, grown for its edible fruit.

Wine growers prune severely each winter to turn the vines into more-or-less compact bushes, sacrificing quantity of fruit for high-quality juice. In the garden, you needn't be so severe; vines can be allowed to grow big enough to cover fences and pergolas. Grapes bear their fruit on shoots that grow from the base of last summer's growth, and the pruning of an established vine is simple—in winter, cut all of last year's branches back to the main framework. How close depends on the variety; the majority (including just about all the wine varieties and most of the best table grapes) are cut back to two buds (spur pruning); a few are left longer, to say ten or twelve buds (long-cane pruning). If you have a choice, choose a variety suitable for spur pruning; it's simpler to manage.

The grape vine is long lived; take time to train it carefully and be prepared to wait until the third summer for your crop. The job may take a year or two longer on a pergola, as you want a clear stem the height of the pergola posts, but the procedure is the same. After some years, you may find the vine's arms losing vigour; select strong shoots from near the trunk to train as replacements and remove the old ones. An old, overgrown vine can be renewed by cutting it as hard as you please in winter and then selecting and training the strongest of the resultant shoots. This will result in your having no crop for a year or two, however.

Propagation Easy, by hardwood cuttings in late autumn

GRAPE VINES

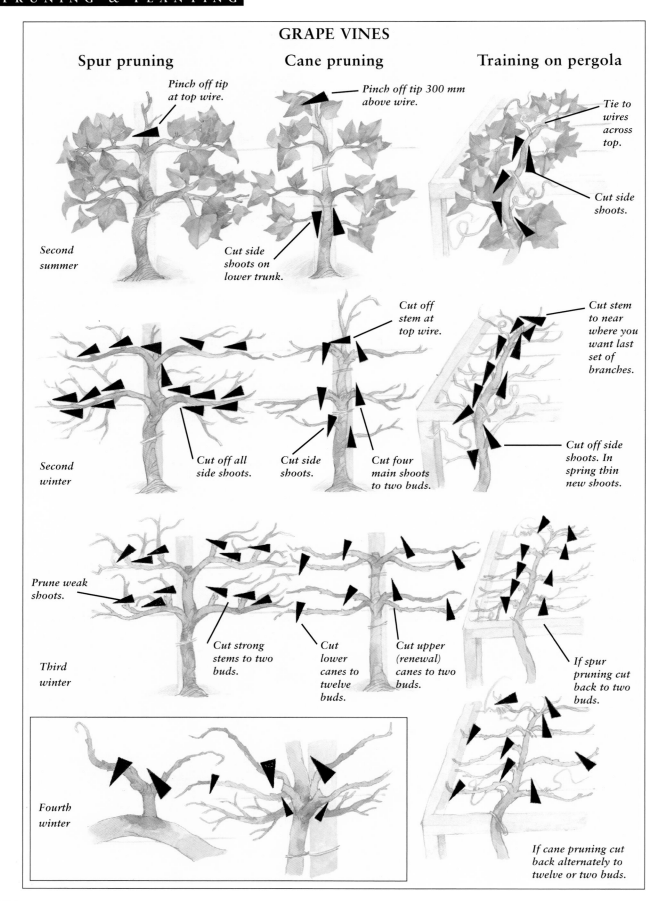

Spur pruning

Cane pruning

Training on pergola

Pinch off tip at top wire.

Pinch off tip 300 mm above wire.

Tie to wires across top.

Cut side shoots.

Cut side shoots on lower trunk.

Second summer

Cut off stem at top wire.

Cut stem to near where you want last set of branches.

Cut off all side shoots.

Cut side shoots.

Cut four main shoots to two buds.

Cut off side shoots. In spring thin new shoots.

Second winter

Prune weak shoots.

Cut strong stems to two buds.

Cut lower canes to twelve buds.

Cut upper (renewal) canes to two buds.

If spur pruning cut back to two buds.

Third winter

Fourth winter

If cane pruning cut back alternately to twelve or two buds.

or winter. In areas where phylloxera is a threat, it is better to graft in early spring onto a resistant rootstock; you can graft an old vine over to a more desirable variety if you wish—wine growers do it all the time so they do not have to wait for young plants to grow.

GUINEA FLOWER
Hibbertia
Evergreen vines or small, bushy shrubs, flowering from spring onwards.

Shrubby types such as *H. asterotricha* need little pruning; if you want to enhance bushiness, trim lightly after bloom. *H. scandens* is a small, shrubby vine. On a trellis, it needs only routine training and occasional thinning to keep it from becoming tangled. Used as a groundcover, it needs occasional heading back to keep it flat and within bounds. The best time for pruning is late winter or early spring before growth begins.
Propagation Fairly easy, by layering of half-ripe cuttings in late summer.

HONEYSUCKLE
Lonicera
Evergreen, twining vines flowering in summer or deciduous shrubs flowering during winter and spring.

The vining honeysuckles vary from rampant to moderate and shrubby in habit; all can be kept under control by heading back out-of-bounds shoots at any time and carrying out more drastic thinning and cutting back after flowering. The Burmese honeysuckle (*L. hildebrandiana*) is a huge grower and usually needs fairly severe discipline to keep it under control. Don't cut it in winter, as it is rather tender. Shrubby species such as *L. fragrantissima* make thickets of growth; prune as for mock orange (see Shrubs). They can be clipped as hedges if desired, but the quantity of bloom will suffer from this treatment.
Propagation Very easy, by layering in summer or by taking half-ripe cuttings at the same time. The shrubby species grow easily from hardwood cuttings taken in late autumn.

HOYA
Hoya
Evergreen climbers, flowering during spring.

Hoyas bear their flowers on short spurs, which continue to flower each year for several years. Don't pick them, and if you want to shorten over-long growth make sure you aren't cutting away any flowering growth; the best time to do any pruning is when the plants are in bloom so that you can see just what you are doing.
Propagation Fairly easy, by half-ripe cuttings in summer or by layering at the same time. Young plants often take their time about flowering.

IVY
Hedera
Fast growing, evergreen climbers, grown mainly for their foliage; autumn flowers are not exciting.

Ivy clings by itself and is a fine plant for covering walls. It also makes a first-rate groundcover. Prune at any time to keep plants under control, but severe pruning is best in early spring before growth begins.

Few climbers suit a rustic fence more than honeysuckle. This is Lonicera japonica, *a rampant grower. Prune it quite severely after bloom to keep it from taking over.*

Hoyas rarely grow dense enough to hide a wall, but the flowers are beautiful.

Young plants benefit from pinching to encourage them to branch and not run straight up to the top of their supports. Trim off shoots that are growing out from the wall and looking untidy, and cut away any shoots that are threatening to grow over windows or up into eaves. You may need to do this several times during the growing season. Old plants tend to build up a mass of growth, which can be severely pruned back to the main framework of stems or even almost to the ground if need be. (If you have to tackle a massively overgrown ivy, wear a bandana over your mouth—the plants accumulate a great deal of unpleasant dust from dead leaves.) When ivy has filled its allotted space, it makes bushy flowering growth, usually at the top of the plant. This has different leaves from the rest of the plant and bears tiny green flowers, followed by black berries. If you dislike them, trim them off. The smaller-leaved, more restrained varieties such as 'Needlepoint' and 'Pittsburgh' can be used for topiary—make up a support from wood and wire in the shape you want and train the ivy to cover it, clipping as needed to keep the outline clean. Groundcovers only need trimming to curtail their spread. After a few years, growth tends to mound up: cut back hard in early spring—new growth will soon cover scars.

Propagation Easy, by layering in summer or softwood cuttings (which will root in a glass of water) at the same time. Cuttings of the mature, flowering growth strike more slowly. They will give plants that always remain bushy and never climb. Such 'arborescent ivy' is useful for knee-high hedges,

and can be trimmed to keep it dense. With patience, you can train it as a standard also.

JASMINE
Jasminum
Mostly evergreen vines, flowering in spring.
The jasmines fall into two classes—vigorous, twining vines with white, scented flowers, and thicketing shrubs, mostly with yellow flowers. The climbing types need the usual discipline for climbers and can be headed back quite severely after bloom if needed (the popular *J. polyanthum* follows its display with weeks of dead flowers and looks unsightly unless you remove them). Also see Shrubs: Jasmine.
Propagation Very easy, by layering in summer. If you want a lot of plants, you can take half-ripe cuttings in summer.

KANGAROO VINE
Cissus
Fast growing, evergreen vines.
Prune these rampant vines to prevent them taking over the garden. Cut out unwanted growth and head back overlong shoots at any time. If necessary, you can cut the plant back to its main branches in early spring. They make good groundcovers in frost-free climates; cut back any shoots growing out of bounds.
Propagation Easy, by layering in summer or cuttings of young shoots at almost any time during warm weather.

KIWI FRUIT, Chinese
gooseberry
Actinidia chinensis
Fast growing, deciduous vines, flowering in spring.
This rampant, twining vine needs annual winter pruning to keep it within bounds and to encourage heavy crops of fruit.

The procedure is similar to that for cane-pruned grapes; the vine bears fruit on shoots growing from wood formed the previous summer. The young plant is trained to one or two trunks and several main branches. If you have a plant with both sexes grafted on it, make sure you don't accidentally prune off one or the other. Established plants are pruned by cutting back the shoots that fruited the past summer to two or three buds beyond the fruit stalks; shoots that bore no fruit are cut back to three buds. Cut out weak or badly tangled growth and remove a few of the oldest fruiting shoots each year to encourage new fruiting growth. Male vines can be treated similarly, but there is no need to be so precise; if you cut away a little flowering wood by mistake, there should still be sufficient flowers to pollinate the females. Shoots that threaten to grow out of bounds can be headed back during the summer months.
Propagation Fairly easy, by cuttings in winter.

MOONFLOWER
Ipomoea alba, syn.
Calonyction aculeatum
Fast growing, evergreen vine.
A tropical vine, the moonflower grows like mad and usually needs some trimming back of wayward shoots to keep it in bounds. In temperate areas, it loses a lot of foliage and looks tatty in winter, but don't trim until the weather warms up in spring. In cool areas, it is apt to be killed back by frost. Sometimes it will come back from the base, sometimes not; but it can be grown as an annual.
Propagation Easy, from seed in spring.

An ivy topiary is trained by running the main stem up a stake and winding the branches around a wire frame. Then you clip to maintain the shape of your 'standard' ivy.

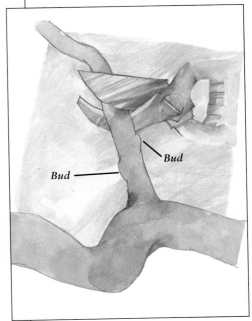

Bud

Bud

Prune kiwi fruit annually to increase fruit. Cut back last summer's growth to two or three buds on shoots that have fruited, to three on others.

Splendid as they can look, ivy and Virginia creeper need regular discipline when allowed to grow on houses. They won't damage sound masonry, but they will find their way into any cracks and make matters worse. This Parthenocissus tricuspidata, variously called Virginia creeper or Boston ivy, is at Stradbroke, Woodville, NSW.

This star jasmine has escaped from its arch and is growing up into an adjacent tree. It would do no harm to cut away the excess growth if you disliked the effect.

PASSIONFRUIT
Passiflora

Fast growing, evergreen vines, clinging by tendrils and flowering in summer.

These rampageous vines need annual pruning if they aren't to become a mass of tangled growth with few flowers or fruit. Those grown for fruit (*P. edulis, P. mollisima, P. quadrangularis*) are best trained from youth to only four or five main branches; in early spring thin out dead and feeble shoots, cutting strong laterals back to 40 cm or so, to encourage strong new growth that will bear the most fruit. Treat the purely decorative types such as *P. caerulea* and *P. coccinea* similarly, but you probably won't want to be quite so severe. If these become a hopeless tangle, try cutting them almost to the ground in early spring.

Propagation Easy, from fresh seed sown in summer; most types will flower within twelve months. Some seedlings can be very shy to fruit and should be discarded as soon as this becomes apparent. Named fruiting varieties are often grafted in summer onto seedling stock selected for resistance to fusarium wilt and are a better bet than seedlings. Ornamental forms are sometimes grafted but they layer easily in summer and can also be grown from half-ripe cuttings at the same time.

POTATO VINE
Solanum

Fast growing, evergreen or deciduous vines, flowering from spring to autumn.

Both the evergreen *S. jasminoides* and the bulkier stemmed, deciduous *S. wendlandii* are used to cover fences and verandas, but they can

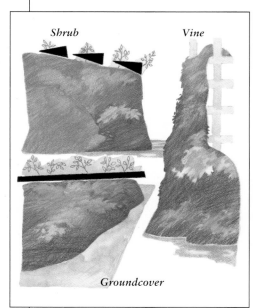

Shrub   Vine

Groundcover

Star jasmine can be grown as a shrub, vine or groundcover. Prune selectively for the effect you want.

Sweet peas flower best when planted close together and trained straight up a trellis. They love rich soil.

become straggly, overgrown and untidy. At the end of winter cut back as severely as you need to—bare wood sprouts easily and quickly. During the growing season, cut back any shoots that are growing out of hand. Both species make unusual, attractive standards; the stem can be 1 to 2 m tall. Train as for wisteria (see below), but keep the stake in place permanently, as the stem never becomes strong enough to be self-supporting.

Propagation Very easy, by layering or half-ripe cuttings in spring or summer.

PURPLE TRUMPET VINE
Clytostoma callistegiodes, syn. *Bignonia violacea*
Evergreen, summer flowering vine. Related to the wonga-wonga vine, it is treated the same way.

RANGOON CREEPER
Quisqualis indica
Fast growing, evergreen vine, flowering in summer.
This grows as a smallish shrub for its first couple of years. Don't prune young plants—wait until a great shoot arises and the plant starts to climb and then you can clear away the original branches. Once the plant is established, it needs routine training. In early spring, before growth begins, thin out weak growth and head back over-long branches. You can prune quite hard, even cutting almost to the ground if necessary.

Propagation Easy, by layering or by taking softwood cuttings in early summer.

SKY FLOWER
Thunbergia
Evergreen, twining vines, flowering in spring or summer.
Most species are sub-tropical perennials that need only the usual vine thinning (in early spring or after bloom) or heading back should they grow out of bounds (at almost any time). An out-of-hand plant can be rejuvenated by cutting it almost to the ground in early spring, but there won't be much flower that year.

Propagation Easy, by layering in spring or summer, or from softwood or half-ripe cuttings in summer.

STAR JASMINE
Trachelospermum jasminoides
Fast growing, bushy, evergreen twining climber, flowering in late spring and summer.
Grow the star jasmine as a climber, a sprawling, metre-tall shrub or groundcover. Trained on a low fence, it grows dense enough to make a small hedge. It can take hard pruning but rarely needs it. As a vine, it can be allowed to grow as it pleases on a trellis: it usually gives good top-to-bottom coverage without special attention. Once it has covered its allotted space, keep it in bounds by heading back the long shoots that develop after bloom. To grow it as a shrub or groundcover, pinch the young plants for bushiness and keep those long shoots pinched back well.

Propagation Easy, by layering or by taking half-ripe cuttings in summer.

SWEET PEA
Lathyrus
Annual or perennial vines, flowering in spring or summer.
Sweet peas can be grown in two ways—allow them to grow as they please, removing spent flowers regularly to prolong bloom, or pinch out side shoots as they develop, confining the plant to one or two stems, which gives the finest, exhibition-quality flowers on long stems. The perennial species such as *L. latifolius* and *L. pubescens* tend to die back in late autumn, when they can be cut back hard for neatness. They will grow back in the following year.

Propagation Easy, from seed sown in autumn or early spring. Germination is faster if seeds are soaked in warm water for a few hours before sowing. The perennial species can also be divided in autumn when the weather is cooler.

TURQUOISE BERRY VINE
Ampelopsis brevipedunculata, syn. *Vitis heterophylla*
Fast growing, deciduous climber, flowering in spring.
Control the plant's size by shortening over-long shoots in summer; tangled and weak stems can be cut right out in winter. Or treat it in a similar manner to a grape vine, to which it is closely related. Completely overgrown plants can be rejuvenated by hard pruning in winter.

Propagation Easy, by cuttings in winter.

VIRGINIA CREEPER
Parthenocissus
Fast growing, deciduous vines, flowering insignificantly in spring but grown for their autumn colour.
The various types of Virginia creeper all cling by tendrils equipped with suckers and so can be grown to cover a wall without a trellis; but they are strong growers and on house walls will need watching to keep shoots from growing where they aren't wanted. Cut off unwanted shoots whenever you see them. Any branches that have pulled away from the wall can be cut back at any time to a point where anchorage is secure. When the plant

has achieved complete coverage, you may need to prune more severely each winter, removing surplus growth. You can cut back quite hard and the plants will still grow back very strongly.

Propagation Very easy, by layering in spring or summer or by taking hardwood cuttings in late autumn.

WISTERIA
Wisteria
Deciduous, twining vines, flowering in spring.

Wisteria is a huge grower but can be kept to almost any size by regular pruning. You can even bonsai it and it will still flower lavishly. Limit young plants to one or two main stems and spend the first few years establishing a spreading framework of branches over the area you want to cover—pinching out excess shoots directs energy to the ones you want to keep and allows the framework to develop faster. To encourage growth, prune wisteria in winter. Once the plant has grown to the size you want, most pruning is done in summer, removing the unwanted growth that would clutter the plant and shortening the long whippy shoots that arise after flowering is over to two or three leaves.

The result will be plenty of the short, twiggy shoots that bear the most flowers, and the branch structure will be handsome even when the leaves have gone for the winter. You can train wisteria as a standard or a several-stemmed bush: eventually the main stems will be thick enough not to need the training stakes. Keep watch for the suckers that arise from the very base of the plant and run along the ground, layering themselves as they go.

Propagation This is surprisingly difficult. Try layering in spring, but be prepared to wait for the plant to make its roots. Hardwood cuttings taken in late autumn will root with the assistance of a rooting hormone, but the young plants usually develop slowly. Seed can be sown in autumn, but seedlings may take a long time to flower, and many will be of indifferent quality. Taking root cuttings in late autumn is probably the best method. Nurseries often graft in winter on seedling stock, and so you need to be sure you aren't taking your root cuttings from an understock—and be wary of layering shoots that arose from the roots. Wait for them to flower to be sure they are the type you want!

WONGA-WONGA VINE
Pandorea
Fast growing, twining evergreen vines, flowering in spring or summer.

Wonga-wonga vines need only the usual training and shortening of any shoots that may grow out of bounds. If a plant gets out of hand, it can be thinned and headed back fairly drastically. For the large-flowered *P. jasminoides* the best time is in early spring before growth begins, and for the small-flowered *P. pandorana* the best time for pruning is later in the season after spring blooming has finished.

Propagation Easy, by layering or by taking half-ripe cuttings in summer.

Plant just arrived from the nursery.

Stake, tie, cut back to one stem.

Start training when shoots appear.

First year: pinch tips of plant.

Second year: remove suckers, shorten branches.

Third and later years: pinch streamers, shape head.

A wisteria can be trained as a standard, but it takes at least three years to achieve that result.

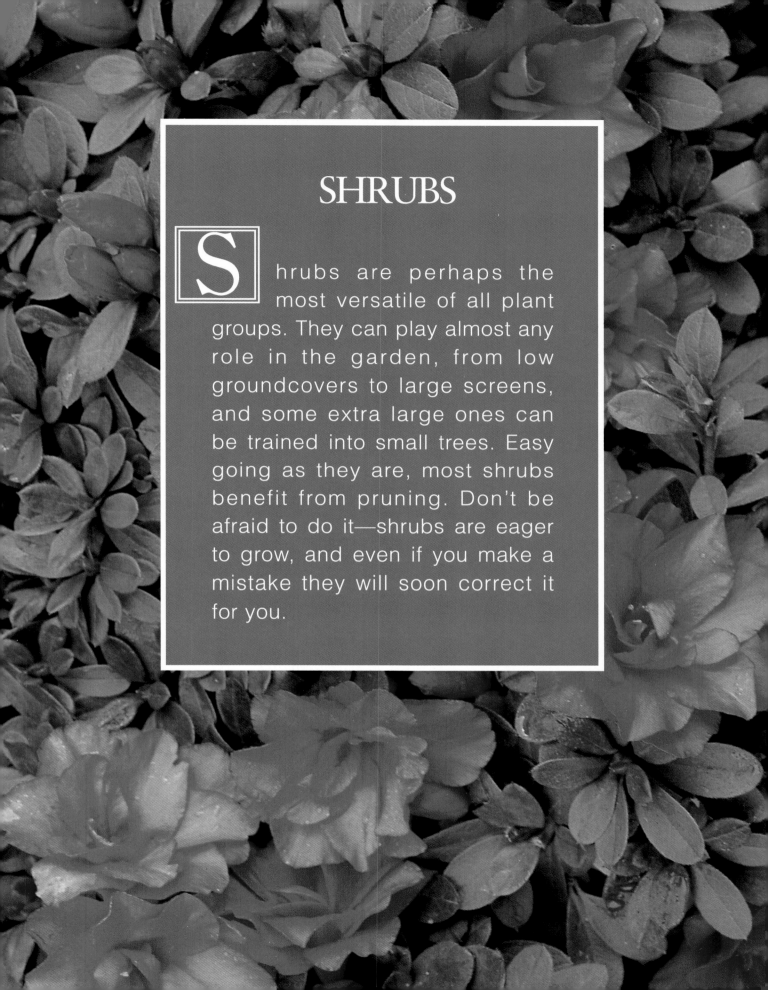

SHRUBS

Shrubs are perhaps the most versatile of all plant groups. They can play almost any role in the garden, from low groundcovers to large screens, and some extra large ones can be trained into small trees. Easy going as they are, most shrubs benefit from pruning. Don't be afraid to do it—shrubs are eager to grow, and even if you make a mistake they will soon correct it for you.

A massed planting of azaleas and rhododendrons. They transplant easily, and if you find you have planted a tall grower in front of a shorter one, shift them around.

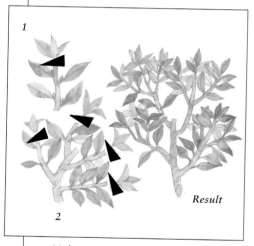

Make an azalea bushy by pinching out new growth.

Bachelor's buttons tend to straggliness (Everglades, Leura, NSW).

This is as compact as you can make Brugmansia suaveolens, *best known of the angel's trumpets. It can be trained as a small tree also.*

ABELIA
Abelia

Evergreen or semi-evergreen, summer flowering shrubs.

Naturally bushy, abelias need little pruning, but they benefit from thinning out some of the oldest branches in winter. Over-long shoots can be headed back to the main outline in summer. Abelias can be trimmed as formal hedges, but this deprives them of their arching grace and reduces flowering. They are not compact enough for topiary.

Propagation Easy, from semi-mature cuttings in summer or hardwood cuttings in winter.

ACALYPHA
Acalypha

Slow growing, evergreen shrubs, flowering uninterestingly during summer months.

Large, dense shrubs, acalyphas can be pinched or headed back for bushiness or to control their size at almost any time (in cool areas in spring). They can be made into informal hedges if desired. An overgrown plant can be rejuvenated and reduced in size by cutting down to about 35 cm in early spring.

Propagation Easy, by cuttings in summer.

ANGEL'S TRUMPET
Brugmansia

Evergreen shrubs, flowering during summer.

All species are large, tree-like but soft-wooded shrubs. They can be kept shrubby by heading back but it is a battle to keep most of them below about 2.5 m. Or train them as trees by removing the lower branches and weak or dead growth; lanky side shoots can be headed back to three or four buds from the main branches. Prune in spring, once

the weather has begun to warm up; they are very sensitive to cold weather.
Propagation Easy, by soft cuttings in spring or summer.

AUSTRALIAN FUCHSIA
Correa
Evergreen shrubs, flowering in winter or spring.
Naturally attractive in habit, none of the correas really needs pruning but young plants will be bushier for a little pinching. To control their size, head them back to lateral shoots immediately after flowering. Don't cut into the bare wood of this plant.
Propagation Easy, by layering or half-ripe cuttings in summer. Grafting on *C. alba,* the strongest grower, is common in Britain but rare here.

AUSTRALIAN HEATH
Epacris
Evergreen shrubs, flowering from spring to summer.
Naturally rather open growing, these can be made more bushy by pinching young plants and trimming back after bloom. Don't cut into bare wood. Replace old and straggly plants when necessary.
Propagation Easy, from spring- or autumn-sown seed, layering or half-ripe cuttings in late summer.

AUSTRALIAN ROSEMARY
Westringia
Fairly fast growing, evergreen shrubs, flowering (mostly) during summer months.
Best known is the white-flowered, neat and bushy *W. rosmarinifolia.* You can begin by pinching a young plant once or twice, and if needed you can trim it after bloom. Shear it as a formal, metre tall hedge if you fancy, but don't ever cut into bare wood. The other

species are less enthusiastically bushy, and pinching and light trimming after bloom are usually desirable.
Propagation Easy, by half-ripe cuttings in late summer.

AZALEA
Azalea
Slow growing, evergreen and deciduous shrubs, flowering during spring.
Azaleas can take quite severe pruning but the naturally shapely bushes rarely need it. Any over-long shoots can be pinched back. The Japanese shear the small-leaved, evergreen kurumes to formal shapes, and over-large plants of the evergreen types can be cut back quite hard in winter to bring them down to size, although this sacrifices that spring's flowers. The best time to prune is when the plants are in bloom; new growth starts immediately the flowers fade. It takes patience, but they make very pretty standards. They are far too bushy to train as an espalier.
Propagation Moderately easy, from cuttings or by layering during summer.

BACHELOR'S BUTTONS
Kerria japonica
Fast growing, deciduous shrub, flowering in spring.
The thickets of stems rapidly become untidy tangles of worn-out and dead branches. You can keep them presentable by removing some of the oldest branches immediately after bloom, or you can rejuvenate the shrub by cutting the whole thing to the ground (again after bloom) every couple of years or so.
Propagation Very easy, by detaching rooted suckers in winter. If the plant is small enough to handle, it can be

lifted and divided like a herbaceous plant, or you can take half-ripe cuttings or layerings in summer.

BARBERRY
Berberis
Evergreen and deciduous shrubs, flowering in spring.
Barberries make thickets of stems and pruning normally consists of occasionally removing the oldest, either in winter or after the berries are over. Head back the others as needed to keep the shrub shapely. Hedges are sheared during the growing season as needed. Renew old plants by cutting virtually to the ground in winter. They have sharp thorns—wear stout gloves and make sure you gather up all the prunings, which can take years to rot.
Propagation Moderately easy, by cuttings in winter or layering in summer. Seed sown in autumn grows well but is unlikely to come true.

BAUHINIA
Bauhinia
Evergreen or partly deciduous trees, shrubs or climbers.
B. galpinii, the coral bauhinia, is a sprawling shrub that can fill up a lot of space if left unchecked. Control it with a combined heading back and thinning operation immediately after bloom; the resulting new growth will usually flower again later in the season. It makes a spectacular espalier subject. The climber, *B. scandens,* is much more vigorous than its dainty foliage and pink spring flowers suggest. It can be kept under control by heading back and thinning out the oldest branches immediately after bloom. Also see the entry for Orchid tree, in the tree section (page 112).

Cut out old stems and shorten overlong branches of blueberry plants.

Bouvardias (this is 'President Garfield') are first-rate cut flowers. Cutting the flowers on long stems keeps the bushes compact and promotes further bloom.

Propagation Usually from seed sown in summer, but summer cuttings and layerings root quite easily.

BEAUTY BUSH
Kolkwitzia amabilis
Fast growing, deciduous shrub, flowering in spring.

The beauty bush needs no regular pruning but can make a thicket of stems more than head high and as much wide. To control its size, cut out a few of the oldest stems and thin out the just-flowered stems a little, immediately after bloom. Hard cutting back at the same time will keep it small but at the price of its arching grace.
Propagation Easy, by hardwood cuttings in winter.

BLUE BUTTERFLY BUSH
Clerodendrum ugandense
Evergreen shrub, flowering during summer.

The blue butterfly bush benefits from thinning out of some of the oldest wood and heading back long branches in early spring; you can also trim after bloom, cutting the spent flower clusters a little way back into the foliage for neatness.
Propagation Quite easy, from half-ripe cuttings in summer.

BLUE SKY FLOWER, pigeon berry
Duranta repens
Evergreen, fast growing shrub, flowering for much of the year.

This big thicketing shrub can be trained as a small multi-stemmed tree by removing the lower branches or can be kept to a manageable size by regular pruning at any time. Cut branches that have borne berries right back to the ground or to a strong shoot that has not yet flowered. Don't just cut branches back;

they will respond with an inelegant bunch of growth. Or you can use the plant as a clipped hedge, clipping after each flush of bloom. It makes a good informal espalier too. Really overgrown plants can be renewed by cutting them almost to the ground in the early spring months.
Propagation Easy, from half-ripe cuttings in summer or seed in spring.

BLUEBERRY
Vaccinium
Deciduous shrubs, grown mainly for their fruit.

Blueberries bear on last year's growth. Remove some of the oldest wood each winter; ideally the bush should have no branches more than about four years old. Side shoots that fruited last year can be shortened to four or five buds, and over-long shoots of last summer's growth can be shortened a little. Young plants can be allowed to grow without pruning until they bear.
Propagation Moderately easy, by cuttings in winter or (easier) layering in spring.

BOOBIALLA
Myoporum
Evergreen shrubs or groundcovers, flowering in summer.

The shrubby myoporums are an exception among Australian plants in that you can rehabilitate an old, straggly specimen by fairly heavy pruning in early spring, but none is long lived. It is probably easier to replace it. The groundcovering *M. parvifolium* is normally completely flat; if the odd branch grows upward, just trim it off.
Propagation Easy, from seed sown either when ripe in late summer or in spring, or from half-ripe cuttings in summer.

BOTTLEBRUSH
Callistemon
Evergreen shrubs and small trees, flowering in summer.

Most examples of this large Australian genus are shrubs, some such as *C. viminalis*, *C. citrinus* and 'Harkness' ('Gawler Hybrid') growing into small trees, occasionally with several trunks. Routine pruning consists of cutting out dead and weak branches. For bushiness, the plants can be headed back after bloom, trimming off the spent flowers but not cutting into bare wood, which rarely grows. If you need to cut further than that to control the size of a shrub, cut to a lateral.

Propagation Easy, from cuttings, taken with a heel, in summer or autumn. Seed (sown in spring or summer) germinates readily, but seed taken from garden plants rarely breeds true.

BOUVARDIA
Bouvardia
Evergreen shrubs flowering during summer.

Most of the popular bouvardias, such as 'President Cleveland', are floppy growers and benefit from heading back and pinching after bloom; in mild areas this may mean several times a year. Once a year, remove a couple of the oldest stems altogether.

Propagation Fairly easy, by tip cuttings of the new growth anytime in summer.

BOX
Buxus
Slow growing, evergreen shrubs.

Although all the species of box are naturally dense and shapely, they take shearing like a dream and are among the best of all plants for formal hedging and topiary. *B. sempervirens*

'Little John' is one of the best of the shrubby bottlebrushes, growing only a metre and a half tall and wide and flowering in spring and autumn. Naturally compact, it needs no regular pruning, but trim off some of the spent flowers to encourage more.

There are two types of box here—the dwarf 'Suffrutucosa', clipped as an edging (it's due for a haircut shortly), and the regular tall variety behind the standard roses. Although it isn't yet at full height, the sides are already being clipped.

'Suffrutucosa', used to make low, clipped edgings to flower beds in formal gardens, can be held to about 20 cm high and wide. (The wild type can be clipped low too, but it is naturally a big shrub and better for hedges about a metre high.) *B. microphylla* var. *japonica* can be used as a low hedge too, but as it is faster and larger growing, plan on allowing it to grow at least 35 cm tall. Pinch young box plants to encourage them to bush out right from the beginning or the hedge will be bare at the base. If a box hedge (or topiary) gets too large, cut ruthlessly to the desired size; new growth will soon fill out any bare patches. Severe pruning is best done in winter, but routine shearing can be done any time the hedge is looking a bit shaggy.
Propagation Fairly easy, from cuttings in winter or layering in spring.

BROOM
Cytisus, Genista, Spartium
Fast growing, deciduous shrubs, flowering in spring.
The smaller types need little pruning, although they are bushier and longer lived if trimmed to remove spent flowers after bloom. Taller kinds can be disciplined more severely, cutting back about halfway to a branch or new shoot, and removing dead or spindly wood. *C. canariensis* can be clipped as a hedge, shearing as needed. Brooms are fairly short lived and they are best replaced when they become elderly and straggly.
Propagation Fairly easy, by half-ripe cuttings in late summer or layering in summer. Seed sown in autumn germinates easily and produces better plants, although hybrid varieties will not come true.

BUCKTHORN
Rhamnus
Fast growing, evergreen or deciduous shrubs, flowering (insignificantly) in summer.
The commonest buckthorn in Australia is the Italian buckthorn, *R. alaternus*, a tall evergreen shrub with glossy leaves usually planted as a formal hedge. It can be sheared at almost any time and will grow strongly if you have to cut it into bare wood. (Old or leggy plants can be rejuvenated by drastic pruning in winter.) Left unsheared, it grows to small-tree size, when you can remove the lower branches and thin the crown a little to show off its graceful habit. Watch the variegated form closely, as it reverts easily to the green form—trim off green shoots as soon as you see them to ensure complete variegation.
Propagation Easy, by layering or by taking half-ripe cuttings in summer.

BUDDLEIA
Buddleia
Fast growing, evergreen or deciduous shrubs, flowering in spring or summer.
All the buddleias make thickets of growth, although they can all be trained as standards or small, multi-stemmed trees by selecting leaders and trimming off the lowest branches. *B. alternifolia* flowers in spring on growth made the previous year and is pruned immediately after bloom, cutting a few of the oldest branches to the ground and thinning out the remainder. *B. globosa* can be treated as *B. davidii*, the butterfly bush (see below). The evergreen *B. salvifolia* can be allowed to make a big arching bush but remove a few of the oldest branches every couple of winters. It can be kept smaller

and more compact by heading back after bloom.
Propagation Very easily, by cuttings in winter.

BUTTERFLY BUSH,
mock lilac
Buddleia davidii
Fast growing, evergreen or deciduous shrubs, flowering in spring or summer.
This, the most popular of the buddleias, is best given drastic treatment each winter, cutting the oldest branches out entirely and shortening the rest by two-thirds; left to themselves, these plants rapidly become a mess of weak and dead twigs. Remove unsightly spent flower clusters for neatness and to promote more flowers.
Propagation Very easily, by cuttings in winter.

CALIFORNIAN LILAC
Ceanothus
Mostly evergreen shrubs, flowering in late spring.
Ceanothus vary from ground-covers to large shrubs but all dislike hard pruning. Pinch back young growth for bushiness and remove dead branches, but otherwise go easy, at most trimming back lightly after bloom to keep the plants compact. Never cut into leafless wood. They are not very long lived, and old, straggly plants are best replaced.
Propagation Fairly easy, by taking late summer cuttings or by layering.

CAMELLIA
Camellia
Slow growing, evergreen shrubs, flowering from autumn to spring.
These shapely plants need little pruning. Young plants sometimes benefit from shaping; if they are a bit leggy, you can head back last year's growth to just above its origin. This will

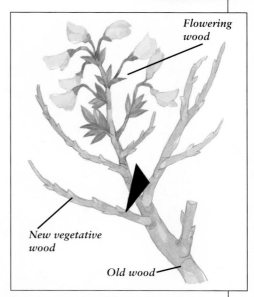

Brooms are pruned by cutting off the flowering wood and half of the new vegetative wood, but they are best replaced when they get straggly.

Prune buddleias in winter by removing the previous year's shoots to two or three buds from the base. If they are left unpruned, they become a mass of weak twigs.

Camellia reticulata *and its varieties (this is the New Zealand-raised 'Wild Silk') tends to be more open in growth than most camellias. Fertilising, mulching and summer watering will do more for them than will pruning.*

produce several new shoots; random cuts usually only give one or two. Older bushes benefit from the occasional clearing out of light-starved twigs that can clutter up the centre of the bush. Camellias respond vigorously to heavy pruning and an overgrown or straggly bush cut back severely in winter will grow back bushy and shapely, although certainly at the cost of a season or two of bloom. Camellias are quite excellent espaliers and the Japanese use them for clipped hedges. Best pruning time is towards the end of the flowering period, before new growth begins.

C. chrysantha, the yellow camellia, is temperamental and prone to die-back; be sure to cut any dying wood back to a healthy lateral.

C. japonica, the common camellia, ultimately reaches 5 m high and wide but can be kept to 2 m or so by regular pruning. Some varieties tend to set more flower buds than they can open properly, and thinning may be needed (some bud drop may occur naturally). You may also want to thin clusters of buds for larger, exhibition quality blooms, the rule of thumb being to leave one bud to each 10 cm or so of stem. Many double-flowered varieties hang onto their dead flowers and need regular grooming to remain presentable. Ask if your choice is 'self grooming'.

C. reticulata, being naturally tall and open growing, is less responsive to pruning and so don't try too hard to make them bushy. (Hybrids with *C. japonica* are bushier.) No need to thin the buds as the flowers are enormous anyway.

C. sasanqua is the fastest growing species. Sasanquas can be leggy when young but you don't need the bother of correcting this; they will fill out in time. Train mature plants as trees by judicious removal of lower branches. They make excellent subjects for espalier and hedges.

C. sinensis is the tea plant. Commercial tea growers prune hard several times a year to ensure a constant supply of new leaves and no flowers. In the garden, prune only for bushiness or to control the plant's size.

C. williamsii plants are hybrids of *C. japonica* and *C. saluenensis*. They are faster growing than the japonicas but are treated similarly. Most are self-grooming and don't need their buds thinned.

Propagation Fairly easy, from semi-mature cuttings at midsummer, but cuttings will root (taking their time about it, however) in a greenhouse at any time. Grafting, usually on *C. sasanqua* stock, is normal for *C. reticulata* and all its hybrids. Only bother with seed, sown as soon as it is ripe, if you want to create new varieties, as seedlings will take five years or more to flower.

Standard camellias look best when grown on fairly long stems, 2 m or so, which calls for patience in the early training. This is an unnamed sasanqua, at Craig Dhu, Sydney.

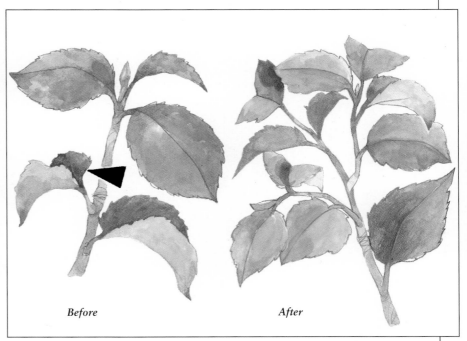

Before　　　　　*After*

A bushy camellia can be produced by cutting just above the scar where one year's growth stopped and the next started. This gives you several new shoots: cutting at random usually only produces one—and no improvement.

CESTRUM
Cestrum
Fast growing, evergreen shrubs, flowering in summer.

The scentless *C. aurantiacum*, *C. elegans* and 'Newelii' are very floppy and best trained as informal espaliers. Pinch tips of young shoots to encourage bushiness and head back about halfway after bloom. Every couple of years, remove some of the oldest, twiggiest stems right to the ground. Also see Night-scented jessamine.
Propagation Easy, by cuttings of half-ripe growth in summer. *C. parqui* comes up readily from self-sown seed and is inclined to make a pest of itself. (In some states it has been declared a noxious weed.) It's better to grow night-scented jessamine instead.

CHERRY PIE, heliotrope
Heliotropium
Fast growing, evergreen shrubs, flowering from spring to autumn.
Pinch young plants several times for bushiness and shorten any over-long branches in summer. You can cut established plants back halfway in early spring, but wait until all risk of frost is over. Standard heliotropes, their stems about 45 cm tall, were Victorian favourites. Train them in the usual way, starting in the spring. Where there is danger of frost, lift them, pot them up and bring them into a sunroom or greenhouse for the winter.
Propagation Easy, by softwood cuttings or by layering in summer months.

CHINESE LANTERN,
flowering maple
Abutilon
Fast growing, evergreen, summer flowering shrubs.
These are more compact if cut back halfway in winter. Pinch young growth in spring to encourage bushiness and more flowers. Rejuvenate old plants by cutting the oldest stems right to the ground in winter, heading the remainder by about two-thirds. Most of these plants are sufficiently flexible in growth to make good informal espaliers.
Propagation Easy, by taking tip cuttings or by layering in spring and summer.

CONVOLVULUS
Convolvulus
Evergreen shrubs or groundcovers, flowering in summer.
C. cneorum is a small silver-leaved shrub. To keep it bushy, head it back about halfway in late winter and pinch the new growth in spring. It is most compact in sun; in shade it tends to straggle. *C. mauritanicus* is a sprawling groundcover. It does not need any regular grooming but is densest if young plants are pinched a couple of times. If it grows over a path, you can trim its edges at any time of the year.
Propagation Easy. *C. cneorum* strikes readily from softwood cuttings in late spring and summer; *C. mauretanicus* will grow from cuttings or is easily layered in summer.

COPROSMA
Coprosma
Fast growing, evergreen shrubs or groundcovers.
C. kirkii is a spreading groundcover. To keep it low and neat, shear in spring and summer, selectively thinning branches at the edge of the planting to avoid a hard, artificial look. Also see Mirror plant.
Propagation Very easy, by layering at any time during the warm months. Half-ripe cuttings can also be taken during the warmer months.

COTONEASTER
Cotoneaster
Evergreen shrubs and groundcovers, flowering in spring but mainly grown for their bright autumn/winter berries.
The groundcovering species (*C. dammeri*, *C. horizontalis*, *C. microphylla*) need no pruning, other than restraining them if they grow out of bounds. Don't just cut them back, or you will get an unattractive hedge-like build-up of new growth—take out whole branches back to laterals some way from the edge. Planted at the base of a wall, *C. horizontalis* will grow up into an informal espalier with little assistance needed.

Larger growers, such as *C. franchetii* and 'Cornubia', reach the size of small trees and can be most attractive with their lower branches removed and some selective thinning to show off their graceful habit (do the trimming in winter), but they really require very little pruning other than regular removal of dead wood. They make good hedges, but clipping will reduce the crop of berries. Start clipping young, or the hedge will not become dense. Neglected and overgrown cotoneasters (including groundcovers) can be renewed by cutting them back heavily in winter; they will regrow strongly from old wood. But the price may be no berries for a couple of years.
Propagation Easy, by layering or taking cuttings in late summer. Autumn-sown seed will germinate freely in spring (it needs the exposure to cold) but won't always come true. Self-sown seedlings often appear and can be a nuisance; birds spread them from suburban gardens to bushland areas.

CREPE MYRTLE,
pride of India
Lagerstroemia indica
Fast growing, deciduous shrub or small tree, flowering in summer. Although it is traditional to cut crepe myrtles back hard in winter to force long rod-like branches bearing huge trusses of bloom (pollarding them, in fact), this completely ruins their graceful shape. They really look best left unpruned and allowed to grow into multi-trunked trees, and they will still cover themselves with flowers, albeit in smaller clusters. Early training will give a single-trunked tree if you prefer. You may need to remove dead branches occasionally. Try not to cultivate deeply around them; they are apt to sucker if the roots are cut. The dwarf strains that grow only a metre or so tall can be cut hard in winter if you wish.
Propagation Easy, by hardwood cuttings in winter or half-ripe cuttings in summer.

CROTON
Codiaeum variegatum
Evergreen shrub, often grown as indoor plant.
Indoor plants can be cut back to just above the lowest pair of leaves in spring if they get leggy. Outside in sub-tropical climates, pinch tips of young plants to encourage branching. Established plants can be headed back to side branches or to pairs of leaves at any time from spring to autumn. Old plants can be rejuvenated by hard pruning but not all at once; first cut back about half the stems, and once they have started to regrow strongly, do the others. With regular heading back, crotons make excellent semi-formal hedges.
Propagation Easy, by tip or half-ripe cuttings in summer.

Although it is usual to cut crepe myrtles hard in winter, unpruned plants develop into graceful small trees which—as this one shows—flower lavishly each year.

Convolvulus mauretanicus *trails slender stems and mauve flowers over a timber retaining wall. If it trails too far, it can be headed back in early spring.*

CROWN OF THORNS
Euphorbia milii
Mainly evergreen spiny shrub, peak flowering in spring.
The crown of thorns is a sprawling, viciously thorny shrub that needs only occasional heading back to keep it within bounds. Do this after bloom and wear stout gloves. The milky sap should also be avoided—it can be very irritating to the skin and eyes.
Propagation Easy, by cuttings in summer. Leave the cuttings out of the ground (and out of the sun) for a day or so after cutting for the sap to congeal before inserting them.

CURRANTS
Ribes nigrum and *R. sativum*
Deciduous fruiting shrubs, flowering in late spring.
Strong shoots arise from low on the currant plant, to bear fruit in their second and subsequent years, but they slowly decline in productivity until they are replaced by new wood. Each winter remove a couple of the oldest branches and shorten the side branches (by about half) on those you retain. Remove any branches growing downwards; they will get the fruit dirty. Black currants bear most of their crop on branches one or two years old; red and white currant branches remain fruitful for longer, and so you retain the old wood longer. Newly planted bushes are headed back hard, to three or four buds, to force strong wood to grow from the base.
Propagation Quite easy, by cuttings of ripe wood in late autumn. Red and white currant cuttings should have the lowest buds cut out, so that the new plant won't sucker from below ground, but there is no need to do this with black currants.

DAISY BUSH
Olearia
Fast growing, evergreen shrubs, flowering in summer.
Most species are neat growers, but pinching young plants will enhance their bushiness and established plants need occasional removal of dead wood. Trim off spent flowers, which will look scruffy. Old plants are unlikely to take the shock of heavy pruning; replace them.
Propagation Quite easy, by half-ripe cuttings in summer. If bushes are branching to the ground, they layer easily, but don't try to bend them too far as the wood is brittle.

DAPHNE, spurge laurel
Daphne
Evergreen and deciduous shrubs, flowering in winter and spring.
Naturally slow growing and shapely, daphnes usually need no pruning other than heading back the occasional wayward branch. The job is best done while the plants are in bloom. Don't be afraid to cut flowers with long stems, as the plants can take hard cutting, but cut to a lateral or a bud that looks as though it is about to grow.
Propagation Fairly easy, by half-ripe cuttings taken in December–January (they root best in sand and warmth) or by layering in summer.

DIOSMA, breath of heaven
Coleonema pulchrum
Evergreen shrubs, flowering in winter–spring.
The compact dome-like shape of the plant is its main asset; to encourage bushiness, pinch young plants and shear established ones lightly after flowering. Old plants can sometimes (although not always) be rejuvenated by cutting back about halfway. The best time to do this is in spring.

Propagation Quite easy, from half-ripe cuttings taken during late summer.

DOG ROSE, river rose
Bauera
Fast growing, evergreen shrubs, flowering in summer.
Forestall straggliness by pinching young plants and heading back established ones lightly after bloom. Like most Australian shrubs, they are not long lived and old, terminally rangy plants are best replaced.
Propagation Easy, by cuttings in summer; they strike best planted in sand.

DOGWOOD
Cornus
Evergreen or deciduous shrubs, flowering in spring.
C. alba and its varieties are multi-stemmed shrubs, grown mainly for their brilliant red bark in winter. As it ages, it turns grey, and the best colour effect is gained by cutting the plants almost to the ground at the end of winter, just before new growth begins—timing is important as you don't want to sacrifice any of your display but you don't want to leave the job too late.
Propagation Moderately easy, by softwood cuttings or layering in summer. *C. alba* can also be propagated by the removal of rooted suckers in early spring.

DOMBEYA
Dombeya
Evergreen shrubs or small trees, flowering in summer.
D. wallichii, perhaps the best known species, will grow into a 10 m tall tree; with early training you can grow it on a single stem, or simply remove the lowest branches as it grows for a multi-stemmed one. It can be trained as an espalier or

over a pergola. The other species are large shrubs, which can be trained to multi-stemmed tree form by removing lower branches. All benefit from thinning out overcrowded branches in early spring, the best pruning time, and from a light trim after flowering to remove spent flower clusters, which tend to persist and look very untidy.

Propagation Quite easy, by half-ripe cuttings in summer.

ELDER
Sambucus
Fast growing, deciduous shrubs, flowering in summer.

The best known elders, *S. nigra* and *S. canadensis*, are both large thicketing shrubs. They benefit from having a couple of the oldest stems cut right out in winter, and you can head back the remaining stems as needed to keep the plant shapely. Alternatively, you can cut the whole plant right down each winter, to gain long rods of growth with extra-large leaves, although flowering will be less abundant. This is the best way to show off the fancy-leaved varieties as their flowers aren't all that profuse.

Propagation Easy, by hardwood cuttings in late autumn or layering in summer.

EMU BUSH
Eremophilia
Fast growing, evergreen shrubs, flowering in spring to summer.

Most species are naturally bushy and need little pruning, although they can be trimmed lightly after bloom. The taller species such as *E. maculata* will take light shearing and make good hedges, but don't cut into bare wood.

Propagation Easy, by tip cuttings in spring and summer or half-ripe cuttings in autumn.

ABOVE: *Most widely admired of the dogwoods is* Cornus florida *'Rubra', a small tree for cool climates. Prune only very gently.*

BELOW: Daphne odora *is naturally slow growing and compact; this old bush has never had any pruning other than lavish cutting off of flowers for the house.*

Prune currant bushes by cutting off the oldest stems each winter and removing any downward growing stems.

Shrubby dogwoods can be heavily pruned—cut the older branches to the ground, head back year-old ones.

This flowering currant is at peak bloom, but already the shoots bearing next year's flowers are in evidence. Some can be sacrificed in after-bloom pruning.

It's difficult to prune this firethorn and keep growth for next year's berries.

The pendant flowers of the fuchsia look lovely raised aloft on a standard.

No amount of pruning will provoke a display of forsythia like this in mild-winter areas, as forsythia needs a cold winter to bloom. There, it is easy and most reliable.

ESCALLONIA
Escallonia
Evergreen shrubs, flowering in spring or summer.

Escallonias vary from metre-tall shrubs to small, shrubby trees, with most being in the 2 m range. All make thickets of stems and benefit from pruning after bloom to keep them compact. Every few years take out one or two of the oldest, twiggiest stems and head the rest back about halfway. They make good informal hedges and can also be clipped formally, although at the expense of bloom. An old, untidy, twiggy plant can be renewed by hard pruning in winter, followed by pinching the resulting long shoots, but there won't be many flowers that year. The very tallest species such as *E. virgata* can be trained as small multi-stemmed trees.
Propagation Easy, by layering or by taking half-ripe cuttings in summer.

EVERGREEN MAGNOLIA
Michelia
Slow growing evergreen shrubs and trees, mainly flowering during spring months.

M. doltsopa resembles the spring-flowering magnolias but is more of a tree. It is a single- or multi-trunked tree, and the only pruning called for is some thinning of the lower branches as the tree matures, to show off the lines of its main stems. Treat the other species, such as *M. champaca* and *M. yunnanensis*, similarly. Also see Portwine magnolia.
Propagation Fairly easy, from half-ripe cuttings in summer or seed sown as soon as it is ripe in autumn. They have rather open root systems which makes them difficult to transplant, and so choose their final positions with care.

FIRE BUSH, powder-puff bush
Calliandra
Fast growing, evergreen, summer flowering shrubs.
Naturally rather spreading and open in growth, the firebush can be made more bushy and compact by pinching the young shoots and trimming lightly after bloom, but don't cut back into leafless wood. Remove dead wood at any time.
Propagation Easiest from seed in spring or by layering in late summer. Cuttings can be taken in summer, but they don't root very quickly.

FIRETHORN
Pyracantha
Fast growing, evergreen shrubs, flowering in spring.
Firethorns can be sheared as formal hedges but at the cost of their bright berries. (The flowers are borne on last summer's growth, which is what you are shearing off.) These big, sprawling shrubs are pruned to control their size. Adopt a two-part strategy: in summer pinch back the young shoots to encourage them to make side shoots that will bear next year's flowers and in winter, after the berries fall, head back the branches that have fruited, cutting back to short side growths. Every couple of winters, cut a few of the very oldest branches back to the ground to encourage new ones to take their place but you can't really make the plants much smaller without butchering them. Where there is room, they make fine, impenetrable screens, and only over-long branches need to be shortened. Firethorns are often recommended for training espalier, but the constant pruning needed is apt to be at the expense of fruiting wood, and as the plants get older the display of

berries gets less and less. *Cotoneaster salicifolia* or even a crab-apple would be a much better choice.
Propagation Very easy, from autumn-sown seed, which usually waits until spring to germinate. (Plants often self-sow.) Layering and half-ripe cuttings in summer, or hardwood cuttings in winter, are easy, too, and guarantee berries in the colour you want.

FLOOR OF THE SKY
Lechenaultia biloba
Evergreen shrub, flowering in spring months.
The blue lechenaultia is so difficult to grow away from its native Western Australia that most people wouldn't dare prune it, but plants will be more shapely and flowery if they are trimmed lightly after they flower.
Propagation Fairly easy, from seed or half-ripe cuttings or layering in summer. They strike best in almost pure sand.

FLOWERING CURRANT
Ribes
Fast growing, deciduous shrubs, flowering in spring.
The flowering currants can be treated similarly to their fruiting cousins (see Currants) but there is no need to take such trouble. Simply cut out one or two of the oldest branches immediately after bloom to encourage new growth. Always cut back to a lateral or right to the ground; stubs will rot. A straggly, neglected plant will usually respond to generous feeding and watering, but you can renew it by severe winter pruning, at the cost of a season's flowers.
Propagation Easy, by hardwood cuttings in winter, or by half-ripe cuttings or layering in summer.

FLOWERING QUINCE,
japonica
Chaenomeles
Fast growing, deciduous shrubs, flowering in late winter and early in spring.
The several species and cultivars all make dense thickets of branches, and pruning consists of removing a few of the oldest to keep the plants from becoming impossible tangles. The best time is just as the flowers are opening. You can control the size of the plants by heading back halfway after bloom, but this makes them dumpy in shape, and if space is limited it is best to grow them as informal espaliers.
Propagation Fairly easy, by taking cuttings of half-ripe wood in summer.

FORSYTHIA
Forsythia
Deciduous shrubs, flowering during spring.
Young plants need no pruning, but when they have reached full size they benefit from having a few of the oldest stems cut out each year or every other year so that new stems will have plenty of room to grow up from the base. Do this immediately after flowering or as the shrub comes into bloom (use the branches in flower arrangements). Old, twiggy plants can be rejuvenated by cutting almost to the ground in winter, although at the cost of sacrificing that spring's bloom.
Propagation Easy, by layering in early summer or hardwood cuttings in winter.

FUCHSIA
Fuchsia
Evergreen shrubs, flowering from late spring to autumn.
Fuchsias flower on their new growth and all the pruning they need is heading back in

winter or earliest spring should they grow straggly. You can cut quite hard into bare wood, the amount depending on how big you want the plants. Pinch the young growth a couple of times during summer if you think the plants could do with a bit more bushiness. Fuchsias can be trained as standards or as espaliers, but it will take a couple of years to achieve the final form.
Propagation Very easy, from softwood cuttings or layering in summer.

GARDENIA, Cape jasmine
Gardenia
Evergreen shrubs or small trees, flowering from late spring and through summer.
Naturally compact and bushy, the florist's gardenia (*G. augusta* and its varieties) needs no regular pruning. Over a couple of years an old, leggy plant can be brought back to bushiness: in early spring, before growth begins, clear out the weakest branches and cut back about a third of the remainder to 20 cm from the base; they should shoot well when the weather warms up. Repeat the process the next

year, and maybe the following one, until the old branches are completely replaced. Don't try to do it all at once; you'll probably kill the plant. The big, tree-like species such as *G. thunbergia* need no pruning other than removal of dead wood. You can remove the lowest branches in early spring if you need to.
Propagation Fairly easy, by softwood cuttings in spring or half-ripe cuttings or layering in summer. The tree species grow well from spring-sown seed.

GERALDTON WAX FLOWER
Chamaelaucium uncinatum
Evergreen shrub, flowering during spring months.
The plants are naturally open and rangy in growth; to make them bushier and promote more flowers, head back halfway immediately after bloom. Don't cut into leafless wood. Other species are less commonly grown, but they can be treated similarly.
Propagation Easy, from half-ripe cuttings in summer. Seed can be sown in spring; seedlings usually bloom in a range of colours.

GERMANDER
Teucrium
Evergreen shrubs, flowering during summer months.
T. fruticans grows attractively without pruning but can be clipped as a formal hedge of any height from about 80 cm to just under 2 m. Pinch the young plants to ensure bushiness, and clip as and when you need. As a single shrub, you can control its size by heading back and thinning out in late winter or early spring. Old, overgrown plants can be rejuvenated by cutting them almost to the ground in late winter; they'll grow back strongly. The less common lower growing and spreading *T. chamaedrys* is more open in growth and benefits from pinching and heading back in late winter; it, too, can make a pleasant clipped hedge.
Propagation Easy, by softwood or half-ripe cuttings or layering, in summer.

GREVILLEA
Grevillea
Fast growing, evergreen shrubs, flowering in spring to summer.
Grevilleas vary much in habit, from prostrate groundcovers

If ever there was a plant that needs regular grooming, it is the gardenia—spent flowers turn brown and hang on. There is no need to remove more than the petals.

Cut spent flower stems back to keep the hybrid grevillea 'Honey Gem' bushy.

such as G. *gaudichaudii* to the silky oak (G. *robusta*), a stately tree. On all types, make your cuts back to a shoot, a leaf or a lateral; grevilleas don't sprout well from bare wood. Many species are most attractive in youth, becoming bare and leggy with age. Replace them rather than trying to rejuvenate them.

The shrubby types need little attention. Pinch young plants for bushiness and cut out dead wood. Over-long branches can be shortened at any time. G. *rosmarinifolia*, G. *juniperina* and some of their hybrids such as 'Poorinda Queen' are useful for sheared hedges and simple topiary, but you must start pinching and clipping young. Some of the types with long clusters of flowers, such as 'Robyn Gordon', benefit from having the spent flower stems trimmed back to a new shoot; the spent clusters otherwise develop into bunches of dead twigs and spoil the appearance of the bush. Groundcover types can usually be allowed to sprawl as they please, although a little early pinching will make them denser. Occasional upright branches on types such as G. *biternata* should be cut down if you want to keep the cover flat. Also see Trees: Red oak and Silky oak.

Propagation Easy, by half-ripe cuttings in summer. Some layer well, and all can be grown easily from spring-sown seed, but seedlings may not come true as they interbreed very freely.

GUAVA
Psidium
Fairly fast growing, evergreen shrub, flowering in summer; grown for its fruit.
The regular guavas are treated in the same way as the pineapple guava (see page 68).

HAKEA
Hakea
Evergreen shrubs or small trees, flowering at various times throughout the year.
Related to the grevilleas, hakeas are treated in much the same way. Pinch young plants for bushiness and remove dead wood as you notice it. Some species such as H. *sericea* and H. *eriantha* are useful hedging plants, but don't try to shear them formally—they don't like too-frequent cutting back. The larger species make elegant small trees; remove lower branches as they mature.

Propagation Easy, by autumn sown seed, or with more difficulty from half-ripe cuttings in summer. The seed vessels go woody when ripe; to get them to shed their seeds, remove them from the plant and keep them in a warm, dry place for a week or two.

HEATH, heather
Erica and *Calluna*
Evergreen shrubs, flowering in spring, summer or autumn.
Heaths have neat growth but hang on to their spent flowers. Remove the spent flowers, cutting the stems to a lateral or a leaf below the flower head, and that is all the pruning they usually need. The taller kinds occasionally send out over-long branches; just head these back. Don't ever cut into leafless wood, which won't shoot; when plants grow old and bare in the centre replace them.

Propagation Fairly easy, from half-ripe cuttings in summer or hardwood cuttings in autumn, inserted in a mixture of sand and peatmoss. Layering in late summer is successful also.

Begin pruning the Geraldton wax flower by cutting the flowers lavishly.

Most of the heaths and heathers (this is Erica mediterranea) *cling to their dead flowers. Trimming spent flowers keeps them bushy, but don't cut into bare wood.*

Autumn sown seed germinates fairly readily in the same sand/peat mix you use for cuttings, although seed of most of the garden varieties won't come true.

HIBISCUS
Hibiscus
Evergreen or deciduous shrubs or herbaceous perennials, flowering in summer and autumn.
The most popular species is the evergreen *H. rosa-sinensis*, which comes in a myriad of varieties varying in size from small shrubs to trees. All can take heavy pruning if needed, but temper your pruning to the vigour of the variety—stronger growers can be pruned harder. The best time is in spring, when the weather has warmed up; don't prune in cold weather when the plant is sluggish. Young plants can be headed back lightly to encourage bushiness; on mature plants you head back by about a third to shape the plant and encourage the new growth that will bear the flowers. Every couple of years, you may want to take one or two of the oldest branches right out. Old leggy plants can be brought back to productiveness by hard pruning, cutting a few of the oldest stems back to the ground and the remainder by about two-thirds; follow up with fertiliser and water. Most varieties can be trained as standards and look handsome that way; and the very largest, such as 'Agnes Galt', can be trained as small, multi-stemmed trees. All can be used as hedges, their height varying with the vigour of the variety, but don't try to clip them formally.

H. *syriacus*, the rose of sharon, is a tall deciduous shrub. You can control its size by heading back, by as much as two-thirds if you wish, in winter; or train it into a small tree with either single or multiple stems. Or you can allow it to grow unpruned except for removing dead branches, and enjoy its naturally elegant habit and pale winter bark. *H. mutabilis* is also deciduous, but less attractive in its habit; cut it back hard in winter to keep it neat and compact. *H. moscheutos* ('Southern Belle' and similar varieties) is a herbaceous perennial. Cut it to the ground at the end of autumn to revitalise.
Propagation Easy, by cuttings. Take them in winter for the deciduous species, half-ripe in late summer for the evergreens. 'Southern Belle' and its kind can be divided in winter.

HOLLY
Ilex
Evergreen shrubs or small trees, flowering in summer and bearing berries in winter.
Hollies can take any amount of pruning to control their size and can be clipped (not sheared, which cuts the leaves in half) to make formal, impenetrable hedges. They are naturally compact and shapely growers, needing little pruning; as they mature, you can train both the English holly (*I. aquifolium*) and the Chinese (*I. cornuta*) as small trees by selectively removing the lower branches. Starved or drought-stricken hollies will develop many dead branches; remove them, and then give the plants a year or two of watering and fertiliser before you decide to prune further. If needed, you can cut them back hard in winter. Don't forget you need both a male and a female to get berries on your bush.
Propagation Fairly easy, from half-ripe cuttings in summer.

HOP BUSH
Dodonaea
Fast growing, evergreen shrubs. Hop bushes can take regular pruning, but being naturally bushy don't need it, except for the removal of dead wood. Upright and dense, they make good hedges, either growing naturally with only the odd over-long branch shortened back, or clipped into a more formal shape. The taller species such as *D. viscosa* can be trained as small, multi-stemmed trees. You can prune at any time.
Propagation Easy, by seed sown in spring or half-ripe cuttings in summer. They strike most readily in sand.

HYDRANGEA
Hydrangea
Deciduous shrubs, flowering in summer months.
Hydrangeas can be pruned after bloom, cutting all stems that have flowered down to a strong shoot, or they can be left until winter, so that you can enjoy the changing colours of the fading flowers. (You get the occasional autumn bloom, too.) I incline to winter pruning—take out any weak stems and cut down the stems that have flowered, either to a strong lateral or to the lowest two or three pairs of buds. Cutting back the non-flowered shoots to a double bud keeps the bush a little smaller (single buds don't give rise to flowering shoots). Prune the white flowered species *H. paniculata* and *H. quercifolia* similarly in winter; harder cutting will give smaller plants with much larger flower clusters. The climbing hydrangea (*H. petiolaris*) needs little pruning. After bloom, cut back the flowering laterals to two or three buds and remove any branches that

are growing away from the support; their weight can pull the plant adrift.

Propagation Very easy, by layering in late summer or hardwood cuttings in late autumn or winter.

INDIAN HAWTHORN
Raphiolepis
Slow growing, evergreen shrubs, flowering in spring.

Naturally shapely, these plants can go through life without pruning, but you can enhance their bushiness by pinching back young growth, or make the plants more open and airy by thinning out small branches from the centre, either in winter or immediately after bloom. They can be clipped formally (shear after bloom) although this deprives you of much flowering wood.

Propagation Easy, by layering or by taking half-ripe cuttings in late summer.

INDIGOFERA
Indigofera
Deciduous or evergreen shrubs, flowering in early summer.

Neither the native Australian indigofera (*I. australis*) nor the Chinese (*I. decora*) needs much in the way of pruning, being naturally neat. Should the plants become straggly, you can cut them back quite hard in early spring.

Propagation Easy, by softwood or root cuttings in summer. *I. decora*, which is a multi-stemmed shrub, can be divided in early spring.

IXORA
Ixora
Evergreen shrubs, flowering in summer months.

Ixoras need only occasional pruning but if they get straggly, you can cut them back halfway or a little more in

Strong growing varieties of hibiscus can be pruned severely in spring.

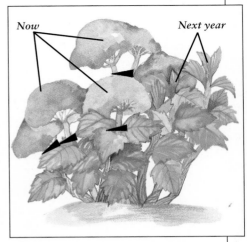

Now   Next year

Cut hydrangeas back when flowers fade, but only branches that have flowered.

Hydrangeas vary in size, the paler varieties being bigger as a rule. Don't try to keep one smaller than natural, or you'll have few flowers. This one is 'Preziosa'.

Holly grows easily from seed, but it is best to take cuttings from plants of known sex—and names like 'Golden Queen' don't necessarily mean the clone is female.

early spring. Pinch young plants for compactness, and remove spent flower clusters to encourage further bloom throughout the season.

Propagation Fairly easy, by layering or by taking half-ripe cuttings in summer.

JADE PLANT
Portulacaria afra
Slow growing, shrubby succulent, flowering in spring.

Perhaps the jade plant might be better described as a succulent shrub; but either way it is able to take any amount of pruning, at almost any time. Usually you need only remove excess shoots to reveal the plant's bonsai-like branch structure and keep the plant from becoming top-heavy. Jade plant makes an easy and unusual, informal espalier, especially in a semi-shaded spot when the shoots will be longer and more flexible than in the sun.

Propagation Very easy, from cuttings at almost any time; fairly large branches will take root quite readily. Insert them in sand, and don't keep them too wet.

JAPANESE ARALIA
Fatsia japonica
Evergreen shrub, flowering in summer; often grown as an indoor plant.

Grown for its handsome foliage, this makes a clump of upright stems. It needs no regular pruning, but if it gets leggy or too tall you can cut the stems back in spring to any point where you want foliage (the flowers aren't all that wonderful). Groom by removing dying leaves and spent flower clusters. Old plants can be renewed by cutting them to about 20 cm from the ground and thinning out the resultant

Lantana montevidensis *is usually grown as a sprawling groundcover, but it can be trained as a graceful weeping standard, as here.*

regrowth. Indoor plants can be treated similarly and it would be a good idea to repot them at the same time.

Propagation Easy, by cuttings of the stems in summer or by air-layering at the same time.

JAPANESE LAUREL,
spotted laurel
Aucuba japonica
Slow growing, evergreen shrub, flowering in spring.

Naturally shapely, these need little pruning. You can control the plant's size by heading back to a junction with another branch or to just above a leaf, in early spring. Variegated forms sometimes revert to plain green; cut out the all-green branches when you notice them.

Propagation By cuttings, which strike very easily at almost any time.

JASMINE
Jasminum
Mostly evergreen shrubs, flowering in spring.

The shrubby, yellow-flowered *J. mesneyi* needs a periodic overhaul to get rid of dead and scruffy old wood. You can either thin out the old branches each year or cut the whole plant back hard every three or four years. Either way, do the job immediately after flowering. The deciduous *J. nudiflorum*, the winter jasmine, is smaller and neater, and needs less attention. Thin out the oldest branches occasionally— if you do it at flowering time, you can bring them inside and arrange them in vases. It makes a delightful espalier. Also see Vines & climbers: Jasmine.

Propagation Very easy, by layering in summer. If you want a lot of plants, you can take half-ripe cuttings during summer too.

JERUSALEM SAGE
Phlomis
Soft-wooded, evergreen shrub, flowering in summer.

Pinch young plants for bushiness and keep established plants neat by removing spent flower stems, cutting a little way down into the foliage. The plants tend to be asymmetrical, with branches of irregular heights; don't try to make them too even. If an old plant is too irregular and leggy, renew it by cutting back hard in early spring.

Propagation Easy, by tip or half-ripe cuttings or by layering in summer.

JUNIPER
Juniperus
Evergreen, coniferous shrubs and trees, randomly branching, and prostrate groundcovers.

Junipers need little pruning. They will take quite hard cutting but not into bare wood. If a young plant is leggy and scruffy, cut the foliage back halfway to make it bushier. Prune in spring. When groundcovers reach their allotted bounds don't just shear them off—selectively take out whole branches, back into the main mass of foliage.

Propagation Fairly easy, by semi-hardwood cuttings in late summer and early autumn. The prostrate types can be easily layered at the same time. Seed can be sown in autumn, although fancy-coloured varieties won't breed true.

JUSTICIA
Justicia carnea
Evergreen shrub, flowering in summer months.

To keep the plant bushy and compact, pinch it when it is young; established plants can be cut back by about two-thirds in spring, once the

weather has warmed up. Remove spent flowers to encourage more.

Propagation Easy, by soft-wood cuttings in late spring.

LACEBARK
Hoheria
Fast growing, evergreen or deciduous shrubs or small trees, flowering in late summer.

Lacebarks are on the borderline between shrub and tree. You can train them to single stems, but their natural habit is to have several stems and they look just as attractive that way. No regular pruning is needed apart from cutting out dead wood and removing plain green shoots on the variegated cultivars. If you want to trim to control the plant's size, do it after flowering.

Propagation Fairly easy, by half-ripe cuttings in summer. Seed sown as soon as it is ripe in autumn germinates freely and grows quickly, but the variegated forms won't usually come true.

LANTANA
Lantana
Fast growing, evergreen shrubs, flowering in summer and autumn.

The wild *L. camara* is a terrible weed which should be pruned with fire and sword but the garden forms such as 'Chelsea Gem' and 'Drap d'Or' are innocuous givers of colour for months. To keep them compact, pinch young plants and cut back established ones halfway in spring. They can easily be trained as standards and look pretty on metre tall stems. Wear gloves while pruning to avoid scratches from the small prickles. *L. montevidensis* is a sprawling, thornless shrub or shrubby perennial used mainly as groundcover on rough banks and the like. It can be sheared back as hard as you need in spring to keep it neat and bushy.

Propagation Easy, by softwood cuttings in summer.

LASIANDRA
Tibouchina
Fast growing, evergreen shrubs or small trees, flowering in summer and autumn.

Most of the tibouchinas are at the boundary between shrub and small tree: *T. granulosa* is usually tree-sized. To grow them as multi-stemmed trees, simply remove the lower branches as they mature. To keep them as shrubs, head back in spring once signs of growth have begun—slightly tender, they don't like being pruned in cold weather. Most can be trained as tall standards, too. Even as trees, they will be more shapely and full of flowers for an occasional gentle trim and removal of dead wood, either in spring or after flowering.

Propagation Easy, by half-ripe cuttings or layering in summer.

LAVENDER
Lavandula
Evergreen shrubs, flowering in summer months.

To keep lavenders bushy and shapely, they should be pruned from youth, but that is not as arduous as it might sound. Pinch young plants and remove spent flower stalks at the base when the flowers fade, if you hadn't already cut them. If needed, cut the foliage back halfway in early spring, but don't cut back into bare wood. Don't try to rejuvenate an overgrown, neglected lavender—take some cuttings and replace it.

Propagation Very easy, from softwood cuttings in spring and summer.

LAVENDER COTTON
Santolina chamaecyparissus
Fast growing, small evergreen shrub, flowering in late spring. Treat the lavender cotton (or cotton lavender) the same way as regular lavender.

LEADWORT
Plumbago auriculata
Fast growing, thicketing evergreen shrub, flowering in summer months.

Left to itself, plumbago makes a handsome billowing mound of flowers but you can control its size by regular pruning, thinning out some of the oldest branches and heading back the remainder about halfway each winter. In cool areas, wait until after the last frost, as new growth is tender. The plants can take shearing and make attractive hedges, but you have to time your shearings for the period immediately after bloom or there will be very few flowers and the young, flowering shoots will distract from the crispness of the outline. You can also train them as informal espaliers, giving them an annual late winter overhaul.

Propagation Very easy, from layering or half-ripe cuttings in summer. Suckers can be detached in spring also.

LEMON SCENTED VERBENA
Aloysia triphylla, syn. *Lippia citriodora*
Evergreen or partly deciduous shrub, flowering during summer and autumn.

This plant tends to be straggly in habit. Pinch back young shoots for bushiness; plants can be headed back hard in winter. Remove dead wood at any time.

Propagation Easy, by softwood cuttings or by layering in summer.

LEUCOSPERMUM
Leucospermum
Evergreen shrubs, flowering in late spring.

Naturally shapely, leucospermums need little pruning. If you cut the flowers, that should be all they need to keep them bushy; if not, you might like to cut the spent flower clusters back a little. But don't cut into bare wood.

Propagation Fairly easy, from seed sown in spring.

LILAC
Syringa
Fairly slow growing, deciduous shrubs, flowering in spring.

Eventually, lilacs become leggy, tall shrubs with all their flowers on top and bare stems and twiggy bits of foliage below. An old plant in this state can be brought back to youth by cutting it almost to the ground in winter, but at the cost of missing out on two or three seasons' flowering. It's better to forestall the need by pruning each year once the plants have matured (young lilacs need no pruning other than snipping off the spent flowers), cutting one or two of the oldest stems almost to the ground, immediately after bloom, to encourage strong new growth from the base. Cut the flowers generously for the house, cutting to a strong lateral; it helps keep the plants compact. Allow a lilac to go to seed, and there may be few flowers next year; but take care as you remove the spent flower clusters not to damage the two shoots that are invariably beginning to grow immediately below them.

Propagation Only moderately easy. Layering in summer is the easiest method. Nurseries usually bud in spring onto the closely related privet. This is

Even the rare lavender, Lavandula multi-fida, *can be trimmed with hedge shears.*

Though most garden lavenders are hybrids, usually propagated from cuttings, they grow easily from seed. L. stoechas, *here, has sown itself around the Adelaide Hills.*

Most of the leucospermums are some shade of coral; selected forms like this yellow cultivar of Leucospermum cordifolium *are best propagated by layering.*

There's little growth coming from beneath the flowers of this lilac. Cut the whole branch to force growth from lower down.

This lasiandra, 'Alstonville', is quite capable of growing 4 m tall; here it has been kept to half that by regular spring pruning. It flowers at the very end of summer.

To renew an old lilac bush, cut the oldest stems to the ground.

The Mexican orange blossom grows in sun or shade—it is more compact in sun, but the foliage is a richer green in shade.

Morning-noon-and-night is a good choice for a matched pair; prune it in spring to keep the bushes the same size and shape without spoiling its habit or flowering.

Prune mock oranges by cutting back vigorous stems to new side shoots.

Don't prune this mock orange yet—the long wands of flowers are not twiggy.

the classic example of a 'nurse graft'—the idea is that you plant the lilac with the bud union well below ground; it eventually develops its own roots and these smother the privet. The privet is too strong for the lilac and if you set the bud union above ground, it will eventually shake the lilac off its back.

LOROPETALUM
Loropetalum chinense
More or less evergreen shrub, flowering in spring.
Much of the beauty of this shrub resides in the grace of its long, slender, somewhat weeping branches, and it would be a shame to trim them back. If the plant gets overgrown, remove a couple of the oldest branches after flowering. It makes a charming espalier.
Propagation Easy, by layering in spring or half-ripe cuttings in late summer.

LUCULIA
Luculia
Evergreen shrubs, flowering in winter months.
Luculias are naturally rather open-growing. Improve their shape by heading back in spring after bloom, but don't cut the whole bush back hard at once—if you need to renew a straggly old bush, do it over two or three years.
Propagation Easiest by layering in late spring, although half-ripe cuttings in summer root fairly readily.

MARMALADE BUSH
Streptosolen jamesonii, formerly *Browallia jamesonii*
Evergreen shrub, flowering in summer months.
The marmalade bush is naturally a rangy, almost vine-like shrub and is greatly improved by an annual trim, either after

flowering or in early spring to encourage it to grow bushier. You can cut quite hard into bare wood if you have to, and if the plant is really straggly with much dead wood it can be renewed by cutting it almost to the ground in early spring and pinching the regrowth once or twice. It makes a very pretty informal espalier or standard.
Propagation Easy, by half-ripe or softwood cuttings in summer. Layering is easy, too.

MAY
Spiraea
Deciduous, thicketing shrubs, flowering in spring or summer.
The big, arching shrub smothered in white flowers in spring is *S. cantoniensis*. It tends to get twiggy and over-bushy with age; open it up and encourage new growth by cutting some of the oldest stems to the ground immediately after bloom. Don't head it back, which deprives it of grace, unless you are clipping it as a formal hedge. It won't flower quite so freely thus, but if you do your main clipping right after bloom you'll still get enough flowers to make a show. The much smaller *S. thunbergii* can be clipped too, although it really needs no regular pruning. The pink may (*S. bumalda* 'Anthony Waterer') flowers in early summer on its new growth. Removing the spent flower heads will keep it compact and often provokes a second crop of flowers.
Propagation Easy, by softwood cuttings in summer.

MEXICAN ORANGE BLOSSOM
Choisya ternata
Evergreen shrub, flowering in spring or summer.
This is a naturally shapely shrub and routine pruning is

only rarely needed. Old plants sometimes become bare in the middle; to renew them, head back some branches by about two-thirds to force new growth and the next year the remainder can be cut to match. You can prune either in late winter or in summer after bloom.
Propagation Easy, by taking half-ripe cuttings or layering in late summer.

MICKEY MOUSE PLANT
Ochna serrulata
Fairly rapidly growing evergreen shrub, flowering in spring.
Young plants benefit from pinching to make them bushy, but as they develop they can be allowed to grow naturally. They do, however, look their best if they are thinned every couple of years to reveal their picturesque branch structure and show off the flowers and fruits. The best time is early in spring, before growth begins, even if it does mean sacrificing some flowers. The plants will take regular heading back to control their size and can be used as semi-formal hedges, although at the expense of character. (Do this sort of pruning after bloom.) Old plants can be rejuvenated by cutting them almost to the ground in late winter but this severe pruning means there will be no flowers that year.
Propagation Very easy, from spring-sown seed—the plant can become a pest and birds carry seeds into the bush. Pull up any unwanted self-sown seedlings as soon as they come up, as they develop astonishingly deep roots very quickly.

MIRROR PLANT
Coprosma repens
Fast growing, evergreen shrub.
The mirror plant is a large shrub. It needs regular cleaning

out of dead wood and cutting back long shoots a couple of times a year to keep it bushy. Neglected plants can develop attractive, irregular forms; clean out the dead wood and see whether you like the shape of the plant before cutting further. Fancy-leaved forms such as 'Marble Queen' are lower growing than the plain green and if desired can be used as groundcovers if you shorten any branches that threaten to grow too tall.
Propagation Very easy, by layering at any time during the warm months. Half-ripe cuttings can be taken during the same months.

MOCK ORANGE
Philadelphus
Fast growing, spring flowering shrubs; mostly deciduous.
Left to themselves, mock oranges make thickets of twiggy branches, and they are neater and more flowery if they are given an annual or every-other-year thinning out immediately after bloom, cutting out a few of the oldest branches to the ground or to a strong shoot. The evergreen *P. mexicanus* is very lax, almost climbing, in growth, and looks very well trained as an informal espalier, with most of the just-flowered shoots removed after bloom.
Propagation Very easy, by taking hardwood cuttings in winter or by layering in summer or autumn.

MORNING-NOON-AND-NIGHT
Brunfelsia
Semi-deciduous shrub, flowering in summer.
The only pruning needed is the removal of dead or overcrowded wood, although if you want to head back the plant to make

it more bushy, this can be done in early spring before growth starts. All the different varieties tend to be more compact in sun and taller and more open in shade. The taller types can be used to make good informal espaliers.

Propagation Fairly easy, by half-ripe cuttings in summer. They root best in sand.

MOUNTAIN LAUREL,
calico bush
Kalmia
Evergreen shrubs, flowering in spring months.

Kalmias will take heavy pruning but are usually sufficiently bushy and shapely not to need it. If a branch grows over-long, cut it back to a lateral and remove spent flower clusters to prevent the plant putting energy into unwanted seed. Snap them off, taking care not to damage the growth buds immediately below.

Propagation Not very easy. Layering in summer is the best bet. Don't be in a hurry—it will take a year or so for the layers to root.

MYRTLE
Myrtus communis
Slow growing, evergreen shrub, flowering in late spring.

Left to itself, the myrtle makes a shapely, bushy shrub about shoulder-high, but it will take shearing (the best time being after bloom) into an aromatic hedge, waist-high or a little lower. If you want to reduce an old plant in size, simply cut back about halfway in early spring before growth begins. Or you can thin the crown out to reveal the lines of the main branches, converting it in this way from a dense plant to a more open one.

Propagation Easy, by half-ripe cuttings in late summer.

NATAL PLUM
Carissa
Evergreen shrubs, flowering in summer months.

There are several varieties, mostly compact shrubs; one, 'Green Carpet', is almost completely prostrate and used as a groundcover. All have the habit of sending out the odd over-long branch, which can be headed back to the main shrub at any time. Otherwise, all that is needed is occasional removal of weak branches, which is best done in early spring. The taller types make good hedges, but don't shear, which damages the foliage— cut the stems back individually to the desired outline. Wear gloves, as the plants are spiny.

Propagation Fairly easy, by layering or cuttings in late summer. Seed sown in autumn grows easily, but only seed of the straight species will come true to type.

NIGHT-SCENTED JESSAMINE
Cestrum nocturnum
Fast growing, evergreen shrub, flowering in summer.

Pinch tips of young shoots to encourage bushiness and head back about halfway after bloom. Every couple of years, remove some of the oldest, twiggiest stems right down to the ground.

Propagation Easy, by cuttings of half-ripe growth in summer.

OLEANDER
Nerium
Fast growing, evergreen shrubs, flowering in summer in temperate regions, almost all year round in the tropics.

The oleander is the classic thicketing shrub, making a multitude of stems from its base, which lean out in all directions to make a spherical

bush. It will grow perfectly happily without ever being pruned, but eventually most varieties need to be restricted in size. Prune in early spring, cutting some of the oldest branches right to the ground and heading back the remainder about halfway, cutting to a strong lateral. If an old plant has got out of hand, cut it almost to the ground in early spring and pinch the resulting shoots when they are about 35 cm long. (Wear gloves and long sleeves; oleander sap is poisonous, sticky and irritating to the skin.) You can also remove the lower branches and thin the basal growths to create a tree with half-a-dozen main stems, but to my eye the branches aren't really attractive. Oleanders make handsome standards and are trained in the usual way, by selecting a plant with a single main stem, staking it and removing any side shoots until you have a trunk about 1.5 to 2 m tall; but they sucker like mad, both along the trunk and from the base. Don't cut the suckers off, or they will sprout and you'll eventually end up with ugly knobs of wood where they originate. Pull them right off, tearing the bark if you have to, and do it as soon as they make their appearance.

Propagation Very easy, by layering or by taking half-ripe cuttings in summer.

OLEASTER
Eleagnus
Evergreen or deciduous shrubs and trees.

The shrubby types such as *E. japonica* need no regular pruning, although their size can be controlled by heading back the long shoots in early spring and they can be sheared as formal hedges. They can be grown as

Mountain laurels grow in the same way as their cousins, the rhododendrons—a whorl of new growth arises just below the flowers. Snip off spent flower clusters without disturbing it. This is a plant for cool climates.

'Punctatum' is typical of the oleanders in being a big shrub—it will grow to 3 m high and wide, even more in hot climates. If you want a smaller shrub, choose the salmon-pink 'Mrs F. Roeding'. It rarely grows to more than about 1.5 m.

This oregon grape, Mahonia aquifolium, *usually only grows to about a metre tall, which is just right for planting next to this picket fence at Fagan Park, Galston, NSW. If it gets above its station, take out the over-long branches after flowering.*

The tiny flowers of Osmanthus fragrans *could pass unnoticed but for their fragrance. It flowers at intervals from spring to autumn; prune after a flush of flowers.*

The orange jasmine flowers several times in summer; to control its size, trim after each flowering.

informal espaliers also. Remove any green shoots from variegated forms as soon as you see them or they will take over. Really large, overgrown plants can be brought down to size by cutting them almost to the ground in early spring and pinching the resulting growth. *E. angustifolia*, the Russian olive, is a shrubby deciduous tree, usually multi-stemmed, although you can keep it to a single stem by early training. Remove lower branches as the tree matures, and thereafter thin out overcrowded branches that obscure the tree's graceful lines. It will take regular pruning and can be used to make a tall hedge.

Propagation Quite easy, by seed sown in autumn, layering or by taking half-ripe cuttings in summer.

ORANGE JASMINE
Murraya paniculata
Fast growing, evergreen shrub or small tree, flowering in summer.

With regular heading back after each flush of bloom, the orange jasmine (so called because its white flowers look and smell like orange blossom) can be kept as a compact shrub from 1 to 2 m tall. It makes a pleasing formal hedge; shear after bloom to gain the most flowers. Left to itself, it will grow to the size of a small tree (4 m or so), when you can remove some of the lower branches to accentuate the lines of its several main stems. If you want to bring an over-tall plant back to shrubbiness, cut it down to less than a metre in early spring, and pinch the resulting shoots. It will flower that summer.

Propagation Easy, by taking half-ripe cuttings or by layering in summer.

OREGON GRAPE
Mahonia
Evergreen shrub, flowering in winter or spring.

M. aquifolium is a naturally bushy, thicketing plant and usually needs no pruning; you can pinch young plants if you like to make them bushier. To control its height, or to make it bushy if it gets leggy with age, cut back as much as you like after flowering. *M. japonica* and *M. lomariifolia* are leggier, their beauty being in their long branches crowned with long, palm-like leaves. Don't try to make them bushy or you'll spoil the effect, but if a plant gets too bare at the base you can cut back the stems to different heights after flowering. *M. repens* is a groundcover, spreading slowly by underground stems, and all the attention it needs is the occasional cutting back of the odd too-tall branch. All these plants can be pruned severely to renew old plants, but it is best to do it over two or three years, cutting some of the oldest branches almost to the ground until the shrub is entirely made of young wood. But the need for all this pruning is rare.

Propagation Easy, by layering or half-ripe cuttings taken in summer. Seed sown when it is ripe in autumn germinates easily but will take several years to flower.

OSMANTHUS
Osmanthus
Slow growing, evergreen shrubs and small trees, flowering at various times of year.

Very little pruning is needed. If young plants are showing signs of straggliness, pinch the young growth to make them bushy. When the plants begin to approach tree size, you

might want to remove the lower branches to show off the main stems. In the orient they are used for clipped hedges. If you shear after bloom, you will still get sufficient flowers to perfume the garden.

Propagation Fairly easy (if slow) from half-ripe cuttings taken in summer.

PAPERBARK
Melaleuca
Fast growing, evergreen shrubs and trees, most of which flower during summer.

The melaleucas vary in habit from fairly substantial trees to quite diminutive shrubs, mostly neatly bushy but sometimes rather open growing. They are all best pruned after bloom, avoiding cutting back into bare wood, which won't sprout. The trees such as *M. leucadendron* and *M. quinquenervia* are mostly short-trunked or multi-stemmed, but by pinching back competing stems you can train them to a single leader. Once the desired form is established, all they need is regular removal of dead wood, although you can impose some control over the tree's size by heading back over-long branches a little each year. The shrubby species are mostly naturally bushy, and this can be enhanced by pinching when they are young and, if you wish, by a trim after bloom. Some, including *M. armillaris* and *M. nesophila*, can be sheared lightly into informal hedges. *M. hypericifolia*, cut back fairly hard in spring, will give long sprays of greenery for flower arrangements. Don't try to make naturally rangy types such as *M. fulgens* bushier than they are—their open habit is part of their beauty. The larger species such as *M. armillaris* and *M. alternifolia* tend to fill up their lower parts with dead brush-wood as they age—remove this to reveal the lines of the main branches and turn them into picturesque small trees.

Propagation Quite easy, from spring-sown seed or half-ripe summer cuttings, which strike best in sand.

PEARL BUSH
Exochorda
Deciduous shrubs, flowering in spring months.

Both *E. racemosa* and *E. macrantha* make thickets of stems that grow up into arching bushes. They can be kept fairly compact by cutting out all wood that has bloomed immediately after flowering, but this spoils their graceful habit and it is better to cut out a few of the oldest stems each year. *E. macrantha* can be trained as a multi-stemmed small tree by removing the lower branches. Neglected plants can be rejuvenated by cutting almost to the ground in winter, but this will sacrifice that spring's flowers.

Propagation Easy, by hard-wood cuttings in winter or layering in summer.

PHOTINIA
Photinia
Fast growing, evergreen shrubs or small trees, flowering in spring and/or summer.

While *P. glabra* in its various horticultural forms is a first-rate hedge plant (regular shearing promotes a summer-long supply of the red young leaves), it is a naturally shapely large shrub, which can be trained as a small tree by gradually removing the lowest branches as it matures and thinning the crown occasionally to show its lines. Left unsheared, it bears more of its small white flowers. If you

want to encourage bushiness, pinch the young shoots as needed. The larger-leaved but shorter *P. serrulata* can be treated similarly, but regular shearing is generally not necessary, and it tends to encourage mildew. It is better used as an informal screen, with pruning limited to the occasional removal of dead and weak branches. Both species can be rejuvenated by fairly hard pruning, best done in winter.

Propagation Easy, by taking half-ripe cuttings or by layering in early autumn.

PIERIS
Pieris
Slow growing, evergreen shrubs, flowering in spring.

Pruning is rarely needed, as these are naturally shapely plants. If you do want to head back or thin to improve the plant's shape, the best time is immediately after bloom. The plants can take regular pruning and are a good bonsai subject.

Propagation Layering in early autumn is the easiest method, but half-ripe cuttings can be taken in summer. They root rather slowly.

PINEAPPLE GUAVA
Feijoa sellowiana
Slow growing, evergreen shrub or small tree, grown for its flowers and sweetly flavoured fruit. (Fruit is more abundant if you have more than one plant.)

The feijoa can be grown as a shrub, with regular clipping as a hedge or as a small tree. To hold it at shrub size, head back the stems after fruiting. It can be trained either as a single- or multi-stemmed tree—for a single stem, select the strongest branch to form the leader and head back the others, removing them altogether when it has reached the height you want;

for a multi-stemmed tree simply allow it to grow as it pleases, gradually removing the lowest branches. Every so often, clear out the weak and dead branches that accumulate inside the plant. It can be trained as an espalier also. Best time to prune is after fruiting, but if fruit is not important to you, you can prune in early spring also.

Propagation Quite easy, from softwood cuttings in summer.

POINSETTIA
Euphorbia pulcherrima
Deciduous shrub, flowering in winter months.

The poinsettia can be allowed to grow unpruned, and in tropical areas it will develop into a small tree. But it becomes very leggy and gawky and most gardeners prefer to prune it hard in spring, immediately flowering is finished, cutting the long stems almost to the main branches. This is really pollarding, and what you have left when you finish is little more than a stump. The result will be huge flowers on long, rod-like stems the following winter. You can pinch the young stems a couple of times, for a more compact, bushier plant, but the bracts won't be quite so large. If you don't fancy cutting quite so hard, you can head back about halfway and thin out the weakest branches, which will give a more natural looking plant with reasonably sized flowers. The milky sap can be very irritating to the skin and disastrous if it gets in your eyes—wear gloves and take care.

Propagation Easy, from cuttings taken at pruning time. Leave the cuttings out of the ground (and out of the sun) for a day or so for the sap to congeal before inserting them.

POMEGRANATE
Punica granatum

Fast growing, deciduous shrub or small tree, flowering in summer. The pomegranate is naturally a multi-stemmed shrub; it looks attractive trained to a single stem, but it will constantly produce shoots from the base and up the trunk for you to remove. A multi-stemmed tree or shrub is less trouble. They look best confined to only three or four main stems—allow all the suckers to grow from the base and you end up with a hopeless thorny tangle. Select those you want and remove the others; you will need to do a clearing out of the base of the plant each winter. You can either allow the plant to branch to the ground or take off the lowest branches to make a tree. Apart from controlling suckers, little pruning is needed, although it is desirable to cut one or two of the oldest branches back to a strong lateral every couple of winters to encourage new growth and keep the plant from becoming crowded. You can head back at the same time to control the plant's size. It's always best to cut back to a lateral; stumps will respond with unsightly bunches of shoots. Pomegranates, especially the handsome double-flowered types, make attractive informal espaliers. The dwarf types ('Nana' and its ilk) need only to have over-long branches headed back during the growing season. Always wear stout gloves and thick sleeves—all the pomegranates are viciously thorny.

Propagation Very easy, by hardwood cuttings or layering in winter. Seed sown in autumn grows easily, but the quality both of flowers and fruits will be uncertain.

No amount of pruning can turn an inferior poinsettia into a good one. More severe pruning would give larger flower heads to this plant, but its scarlet bracts will always be narrower and less impressive than those of the newer varieties.

Don't expect much fruit from a double-flowered pomegranate like this one—but aren't the flowers lovely?

Poinsettias can be cut back heavily but leave two or three buds on each stem. The result will be long stems with huge flowers.

Rhododendron ponticum *is rather looked down on by rhododendron buffs, but it is the easiest to grow in warm climates and its vigour and ease of propagation (by layers or seed) make it the favourite understock for grafting fancier varieties.*

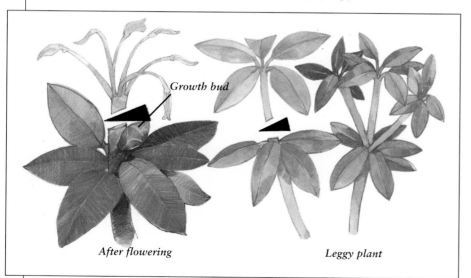

Growth bud

After flowering

Leggy plant

After rhododendron flowers are finished, snap off the cluster, but don't damage the growth bud. Cut leggy plants back to a whorl of leaves.

POMPON BUSH
Dais cotinifolia
Deciduous shrub, flowering during spring months.
No regular pruning is needed, but if the plant isn't bushy you can head it back after bloom.
Propagation Fairly easy, by layering or half-ripe cuttings in late summer.

PORTWINE MAGNOLIA
Michelia figo
Slow-growing evergreen shrub, spring flowering.
A naturally dense and shapely plant, it really needs no regular pruning but can be sheared as a hedge (in spring or after bloom). Old plants can have the lower branches removed.
Propagation Fairly easy, from half-ripe cuttings in summer or seed sown as soon as it is ripe in autumn.

PRIDE OF BARBADOS, bird of paradise bush
Caesalpinia
Evergreen or briefly deciduous shrubs or small trees, flowering in summer months.
No routine pruning is needed other than occasional thinning out of dead, weak or over-crowded wood. *C. gilliesii*, the most cold-tolerant species and deciduous in cool areas, can be trained as a small tree by removing lower branches; if it gets overgrown or straggly, cut it hard back (to about half a metre) to renew it and force shrubbier growth. *C. pulcherrima* is sub-tropical. It is a large shrub to 4 m; to hold it at half that size, cut it back almost to the ground each year. Do all pruning in spring, after any danger of frost has passed but before new growth begins.
Propagation Easiest from seed (soaked in water first) in spring, or by layering in summer. Cuttings do not root easily.

PRIVET
Ligustrum
Evergreen shrubs or small trees, flowering in spring.

The Japanese privet (*L. ovalifolium*) is a standard hedge plant, but it needs constant trimming to keep it looking crisp. It grows back strongly from hard pruning (which is best done in early spring), so you can cut savagely to restore a hedge to shape. Always slope the sides of a privet hedge or it will become bare at the base. Left to itself, it will grow into a small tree and can have its lower branches removed, but there are choicer shrubs for the purpose. The large-leaved privet (*L. lucidum*) lends itself to the same treatment; its leaves are really too big to make an effective hedge. The variegated forms of both species are choicer than the plain green, but you have to remove the frequent all-green shoots or they will take over.

Propagation Far too easy from seed—self-sown seedlings are a major weed in near-city bushland. The variegated forms are easy from half-ripe cuttings in summer.

QUEEN'S FLOWER
Lagerstroemia speciosa
Fast growing, deciduous tree, flowering in summer.

This is a large tropical tree. It needs no pruning other than early training and occasional removal of dead wood.

Propagation Easiest from seed in spring. Winter cuttings can be tried, too.

RASPBERRY
Rubus idaeus and hybrids
Fast growing, deciduous shrubs, flowering in spring and grown for their fruit.

You can grow raspberries as free-standing bushes, but they are really easier to manage if you train them like climbing roses on a trellis. (This stops them trailing on the ground and layering themselves everywhere.) Pruning is simple: immediately after harvest, cut the canes that have just borne fruit right to the ground, to make room for the new ones that have been growing through the summer and will bear next year's fruit. In winter you can shorten these to a manageable length and spur back any side shoots, if you wish. Modify the procedure a little for autumn-fruiting varieties, which bear the autumn crop on the ends of the new canes: simply trim back the sections that have fruited, leaving the rest to fruit again next summer. Afterwards they can be cut right out. Alternatively, you can use a system recently devised in America. This involves cutting the entire plant right to the ground every other winter: in the first year after pruning you get no fruit, but in the second you get a bumper crop. Then you cut the whole plant down again. To get a crop every year, you prune half your plants one winter, the other half next winter. This is certainly simpler; and it is claimed that even with only half the plants bearing at any time, the crop is just as good.

Propagation Very easy, by layering at almost any time or by taking hardwood cuttings in late autumn.

RHODODENDRON
Rhododendron
Evergreen shrubs or small trees, flowering in spring.

Rhododendrons, whether they be tiny shrubs, small bushy trees or something in between, rarely need much pruning. If an over-long branch spoils the plant's symmetry, head it back after flowering. Occasionally you may want to clear out weak wood from the centre of the bush, but usually all that you need to do is to remove the spent flowers to prevent the plant from wasting unwanted energy in seed. This is easy; you simply snap off the whole flower head. No need to cut, but do it gently so as not to damage the growth buds that will be starting into growth immediately below the flowers. The best time to prune if necessary is when the plants are coming into bloom, as growth is usually under way by the time flowering is quite finished. (Use the trimmings as cut flowers.) Unlike azaleas, rhododendrons have their buds in tiers, in the axils of the whorls of leaves. To cut into bare wood, you have to search the stems for the circular scars that mark successive bursts of growth, and cut just above them. A few varieties, such as 'Fragrantissimum' and some of the vireyas, are naturally somewhat open in growth: to enhance their bushiness, pinch back the young shoots after bloom, but don't overdo it or the plant will react with much non-flowering growth. Should you be the fortunate owner of a hugely overgrown, straggly rhododendron, you can rejuvenate it by cutting it back hard in late winter, taking care to make your cuts above growth rings. This can be done all at once, but it is better to do the job progressively over two or three years.

Propagation The easiest method in the garden is layering in early spring; air-layering is successful, too. Cuttings taken in summer strike with difficulty, and before the advent of mist-equipped green-houses most types were graft-ed, usually onto seedlings of *R. ponticum*. Seed can be sown in autumn, but seedlings won't generally breed true and will take several years to flower.

RICE-PAPER PLANT
Tetrapanax papyrifera
Evergreen shrub, flowering in summer months.
This is primarily grown for its huge leaves, although the white sprays of summer flowers are striking too. It grows into a clump of tall stems bearing a bunch of leaves at the top. If you want to keep the foliage down near ground level, sim-ply cut over-tall stems down to any height you wish, and thin out suckers. Or if you want to keep several tall stems for an effect like a clump of palms, remove suckers from ground level as they appear. In any event, you will probably want to remove excess suckers to keep the clump from spreading and engulfing everything in sight. Remove the spent flow-ers for neatness and to keep the plant from diverting energy into seed. Be careful of the fuzz that covers the new growth: it is murder if you get it in your eye and irritating to the skin.
Propagation Very easy, by detaching rooted suckers at any time except in winter. If that doesn't give you enough new plants, you can make sum-mer cuttings from 20 cm long sections of stem.

ROCK ROSE
Cistus
Fast growing, evergreen, spring to summer flowering shrubs.
Rock roses are naturally bushy and there is no need to prune them, although young plants will be better for a bit of pinching. They are not very

long lived, and when plants begin to become straggly and filled with dead wood, it is eas-ier to replace them, but you can keep them going for a cou-ple of years longer by cutting out the dead wood and head-ing back about halfway after bloom. Don't cut into leafless wood, which won't regrow.
Propagation Easy, by cuttings of the young growth taken in the summer months.

RONDELETIA
Rondeletia amoena
Fast growing, evergreen shrub, flowering in winter or spring.
Heading back young plants halfway immediately after bloom will encourage them to grow bushy. Established plants also benefit from trimming off the unsightly spent flower clus-ters after bloom. Overgrown plants can be rejuvenated by hard pruning; this is best done in late winter, sacrificing the current season's flowers.
Propagation Easy, by half-ripe cuttings in summer. Layering in summer is even easier.

ROSE
Rosa
Fast growing, multi-stemmed, deciduous shrubs, flowering in spring or in bursts from spring through to autumn.
If you remember how roses grow, it isn't difficult to prune them. Whether they be bushes, shrubs or climbers, all grow in much the same way—strong shoots rise from the base of the plant, bear flowers for a cou-ple of years, and gradually decline and die, to be replaced by new growth from the base of the plant. Pruning assists the process, by removing dead and senile branches and trimming away top growth that is too weak or twiggy to bear fine flowers, in order to encourage

vigorous new growth from the base. That's basically all there is to it, although the detail varies according to the type of rose. If you are in doubt how to tackle an unfamiliar rose, leave it unpruned (except for removing dead wood) for a year or two to see how it grows. It certainly won't come to any harm.
Roses fall into two main types as far as pruning is con-cerned: those that bloom only once (some time in spring) and receive their main pruning immediately after bloom, and those that flower repeatedly and are pruned in winter. Once-flowering roses include most wild roses (species), the gallicas, damasks, centifolias, mosses and albas among the old-fashioned roses and many (although not all) climbers. They bear their blooms on side shoots from the last year's growth (and from branches two or three years old), after-wards making flowerless, strong growths that will bear next year's flowers. Prune bush and shrub types immediately after bloom, first removing any dead wood, then cutting out one or two of the oldest branches entirely and taking twiggy growth that has flow-ered back to a strong shoot. (Cutting large sprays of flow-ers for the house begins the pruning process.) If the rose is intended to bear hips in autumn, go easier, or you'll be cutting away the hips. The whole operation is not so dif-ferent from the way you prune any other multi-stemmed, spring flowering shrub. You can tidy up the plants again in winter if you like, shortening long, unflowered shoots a little so that they don't wave around above the main outline of the rose bush.

The essential difference between a bush or shrub rose and a climber is that the shoots of a climber are longer and need to be trained and attached to their support—roses don't really climb in the sense that, say, an ivy or jasmine does, and a climber trained on a wall or fence is really a kind of informal espalier. The once-flowering climbers are pruned immediately after bloom, cutting out one or two of the oldest canes either entirely, or back to where a strong new cane shows signs of arising; removing any twiggy growth that won't bear good flowers again and tying in the new branches as they grow. Try to train most of the branches of climbers horizontally or almost so; that way they'll flower along their whole length. Upright, they are likely to bear just a few flowers at their ends. Ramblers of the 'Dorothy Perkins' type are strictly once-bearers—after one of their long, very flexible canes has flowered, it won't produce as well again, and so you simply cut the just-flowered branches right to the ground when the flowers have faded, and then tie the new ones into place as they grow. This is a much bigger job than it sounds, as the new canes are likely to be well on the way and the whole thing is already becoming something of a tangle.

Repeat-flowering roses flower on the current year's growth as well as on the side shoots from older wood and are pruned in winter. The best time is around the middle of July, although you can do the job at any time from when the plants become dormant and start to lose their leaves to when new growth begins. Most roses in Australian gardens are

With cutting back to curtail its size, this rondeletia is getting a bit bare at the base. It would be improved by severe pruning next winter and some fertiliser afterwards.

Admired mainly for its leaves, the rice paper plant can be pruned at almost any time you feel the need, but if you fancy the flowers, delay pruning until after bloom.

Rock rose plants vary in size according to variety, from knee- to shoulder-high.

This bush (hybrid tea) rose has been pruned fairly severely.

TOP LEFT: *Lightly pruned rose bushes need other flowers to hide their bare legs—but what a show they make.* TOP RIGHT: *The new 'English Roses' are best pruned, rather lightly, in winter.* BOTTOM RIGHT: *'China Doll' is a low growing cluster rose or 'patio rose'. Prune it as any other bush rose.* BOTTOM LEFT: *If trimmed lightly in late March or April, 'Lorraine Lee' will flower in winter.*

repeat-flowering bush roses, either large-flowered (hybrid teas) or cluster flowered (floribundas). First, remove all dead wood and then branches that are too worn out to bear good flowers. They have rough bark (young productive wood still has smooth bark) and the spindly side shoots, and either cut them back to a strong young branch or right to the base. This will leave you with a bush made up of branches from one to about three years old. Even these will probably have skinny side shoots or ends: the rule of thumb is that if a stem is thinner than an old-fashioned lead pencil, it is too thin to keep. Then comes the question whether to prune hard or lightly? Hard pruning involves cutting down the good branches to about a quarter of their length, but this method is out of favour—it shocks the plants too much and shortens their lives. Most people now favour shortening the branches by about a third, although in cold areas you can cut to about half. If in doubt, go lightly for a year or two; you can always prune a little harder next time

if you feel your bushes are growing a bit tall and leggy. But don't try to keep a rose bush very much shorter than it wants to grow and don't try to force it to be symmetrical. If it looks a bit lop-sided after pruning, no matter. It will fill out with new growth.

All repeat-flowering roses benefit from regular dead-heading to encourage further waves of flowers. Don't, however, deprive them of too much foliage—leave at least three leaves behind on each stem. If you are cutting long-stemmed roses for the house, you can leave two leaves, but don't take too many.

If you need to renew an old, neglected bush, harden your heart and prune it hard, just this once, in winter. Then water and fertilise lavishly come spring.

You will need to modify this method for some repeat-flowering roses. It is traditional to prune the cluster-flowered bushes more lightly than large-flowered ones; very strong growers can be treated a little harder than weaker ones; and some varieties have wood

slimmer than others, so that the pencil rule doesn't always apply. Those old Victorian favourites, the tea roses, are pruned lightly, by no more than about a third; and repeat-flowering shrub roses such as the new English roses are pruned more lightly also. Some repeat-blooming old-fashioned roses such as the bourbons, hybrid musks and hybrid perpetuals make very long, almost climbing, branches after their first bloom. Come winter, you can shorten these to the main lines of the bush, but you may like to try a Victorian technique called 'pegging down': just tip the shoots lightly and then bend their ends (gently, gently!) down to the ground all around the bush, tying them to neighbouring bushes or to short stakes. They will burst into bloom along their whole length, and the display will be gorgeous. You can try the same trick with the once-flowering roses too. Repeat-blooming climbers are pruned in winter too, and you just tip and then tie into place the long branches. If a flowered side shoot is pencil thickness or

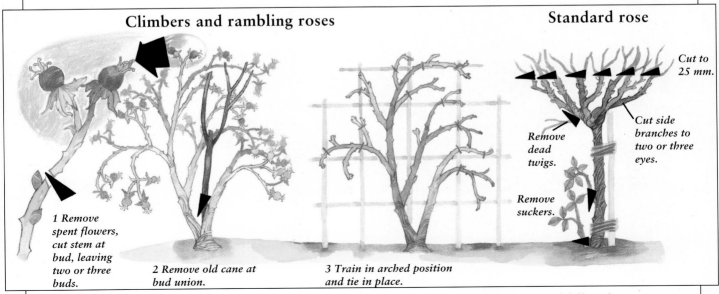

Climbers and rambling roses

Standard rose

Cut to 25 mm.

Cut side branches to two or three eyes.

Remove dead twigs.

Remove suckers.

1 Remove spent flowers, cut stem at bud, leaving two or three buds.

2 Remove old cane at bud union.

3 Train in arched position and tie in place.

There are three main stages for pruning climbing and hybrid tea roses. Standard roses (right) are treated differently.

more, head it back to two or three leaves, and there will be flowers: as a rule the branches of repeat-blooming climbers stay productive for longer than the spring-only ones and they make less wood from the base of the plant.

The miniatures are just very small, repeat-flowering bushes. You can prune them in the same way, but it's a fiddly job. Most won't mind if you simply cut them down to a few centimetres from the ground in winter. It keeps the bushes more truly miniature, too.

Always fertilise roses after pruning, to make up the food that was stored in the branches you have cut away. Finally, if you see suckers from the understock (recognised by quite different leaves from the scion), yank them out firmly. Don't just cut them off or they'll be back.

Propagation Some roses will root from hardwood cuttings in late autumn, although the percentage of strikes is not always very high. It depends on the rose. Most will grow from half-ripe cuttings in summer too, inserted in pots of sandy soil and enclosed in a plastic bag to keep them from drying out. If the thorns snap off easily, the branch is ready. Nurseries propagate by budding in summer, usually on cutting-grown understocks, which have had all but the topmost growth buds excised so that they won't sucker. If you can get the appropriate understock cuttings (from a sucker perhaps), try it—no other graft is so easy.

ROSEMARY
Rosmarinus officinalis
Fairly fast growing, evergreen shrub, flowering in spring.
In its youth, rosemary is a rounded bushy shrub; as it gets older it tends to become either straggly or more picturesque, according to your point of view. Pinching from the start will keep it bushy, and you can improve the symmetry of an established bush by heading back about halfway into the foliage immediately after flowering. But you can't cut into bare wood, and rejuvenating a really gnarled old bush is impossible. Better to replace it or just enjoy its character. The creeping rosemary 'Prostratus' is a sprawler, charming in its waywardness. Don't try to discipline it too much.
Propagation Easy, by half-ripe cuttings or layering in summer. Seed sown in spring grows fairly quickly, but the resulting plants will be variable in habit and flower colour.

SACRED BAMBOO
Nandina domestica
Fairly slow growing, evergreen shrub, flowering in summer.
Unrelated to the true bamboos, the sacred bamboo makes a

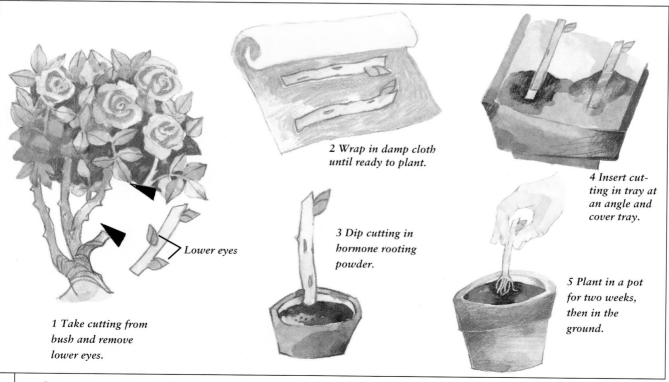

2 Wrap in damp cloth until ready to plant.

Lower eyes

3 Dip cutting in hormone rooting powder.

4 Insert cutting in tray at an angle and cover tray.

5 Plant in a pot for two weeks, then in the ground.

1 Take cutting from bush and remove lower eyes.

Propagating species and climbing roses from cuttings.

thicket of more-or-less unbranched stems, crowned with long sprays of leaves. It eventually gets bare at the base; to clothe its legs, simply cut a couple of the oldest branches down almost to the ground in late winter every couple of years. Spent fruiting stems are apt to remain on the plant for a long time; groom by removing them. If you want to rejuvenate an old, lanky plant, do it in stages. This will probably cost a year's flowers and berries. The dwarf nandina, 'Nana', needs no pruning.

Propagation Easy, by half-ripe cuttings in late summer. Sometimes you can detach rooted suckers, and plants that are not too big to dig up can be lifted and divided in late winter, by cutting the root-stock into sections.

SAINT JOHN'S WORT
Hypericum
Evergreen or semi-evergreen shrubs and groundcovers, flowering in summer.

The shrubby hypericums such as *H. patulum* 'Hidcote' and the variegated *H. moserianum* don't need annual pruning, but they are apt to become leggy. Thinning out some of the oldest stems and heading back the rest about halfway every second or third winter will keep them compact. *H. calycinum* spreads by underground runners and is one of the best of all groundcovers. To keep it dense and full of flowers, shear it back almost to the ground every couple of years, in early spring before growth. It grows fast, and new shoots will soon take away the butchered look.

Propagation Easy, by layering or softwood cuttings in summer. *H. calycinum* can be divided just like any herbaceous plant.

An old sacred bamboo plant can be pruned in two stages, first cutting back half the stems and then the rest a year later.

Its tolerance of regular clipping makes rosemary a good choice for small scale topiary; this one has for understudy a clipped Muehlenbeckia axillaris.

This Saint John's wort, the golden 'Hidcote', is trimmed every winter to keep it compact. It is accompanied by the herbaceous perennial Hosta plantaginea.

The Chinese snowball tree, Viburnum macrocephalum, *is more or less evergreen and less common than the deciduous* V. opulus. *It is treated in just the same way.*

SILK TASSEL BUSH
Garrya elliptica
Slow growing, evergreen shrub, flowering in winter or early spring. No regular pruning is needed. As the plant matures, you can encourage it to grow into multi-stemmed tree form by removing the lower branches. This is a good plant for a flowering hedge or espalier; head back over-long shoots after bloom. Avoid cutting into bare wood if you can.
Propagation Fairly easy, from half-ripe cuttings or by layering in summer.

SMOKE BUSH, WIG TREE
Cotinus coggygria
Deciduous shrub, flowering during late spring.
This big shrub can be trained as a small single-stemmed or multi-stemmed tree by removing the lower branches in winter. The purple-leaved forms are sometimes cut back to stumps each winter to keep them small and force large leaves, but as the plant flowers on last summer's growth, this will mean few if any flowers. Hard winter pruning will renew an old and overgrown shrub. Wear gloves; the sap is sticky and hard to wash off your hands.
Propagation Easy, by half-ripe cuttings in late summer or early autumn.

SNOWBALL TREE
Viburnum opulus
Deciduous shrub, flowering in spring months.
The best known viburnum in Australia, *V. opulus* 'Sterile', is a big, multi-stemmed shrub, and benefits from the occasional thinning out of the oldest branches after bloom. If you want to keep the plant a bit smaller than its natural 3 m, you can head the just-flowered

stems back to a strong shoot each year. Alternatively, you can remove the lower branches as the plant matures and thus turn it into a multi-stemmed small tree.

Propagation Easy, can be grown from hardwood cuttings in autumn or softwood cuttings in late spring; layers readily in summer.

SNOWBERRY
Symphoricarpos
Deciduous multi-stemmed shrubs, flowering in spring and bearing decorative fruits in summer.

The only pruning needed is the occasional thinning out of stems that have fruited, either just after the fruit has dropped or in early spring. The plants will take clipping as small formal hedges, but this deprives them of grace and usually of much berry, too. If the thicket spreads too far, simply dig out or pull up the suckers in areas beyond the limit you have set.

Propagation Very easy, by detaching suckers in autumn or spring, or by softwood cuttings in autumn. You can lift the whole plant and divide it in late autumn, like a perennial.

SPINDLE TREE
Euonymus
Deciduous or evergreen shrubs or evergreen vines, flowering in spring and bearing decorative fruit in autumn.

Deciduous species such as *E. europaeus* make thickets of stems and look best if you thin them a little, removing a few of the oldest, twiggiest branches every other winter. The main evergreen species is *E. japonicus*. It is naturally compact and bushy but in time becomes a big shrub and you can then remove the lower branches, to grow other plants beneath it. (Thinning out some

of the rest will let more light through.) Alternatively, you can cut it back hard in late winter. It will survive regular clipping and can be used as a formal hedge or for simple topiary. Remove any green branches on the variegated kinds as soon as you see them, or they will rapidly take over. *E. fortunei* and its many varieties are shrubby vines, often grown as groundcover. All they need is occasional trimming back if they get out of bounds. You can trim back at any time as needed.

Propagation Very easy, by layering from spring to autumn. Half-ripe cuttings root easily in late summer.

SWAN RIVER PEA BUSHES
Brachysema
Evergreen shrubs, flowering in spring months.

These Western Australian natives need no regular pruning. Young plants can be pinched to help them bush out and you can trim after bloom if you wish, but go lightly. As with many Australian plants, it is better to replace old and straggly plants than to try to rejuvenate them by pruning.

Propagation Easy, by scarified seed sown in spring and from layering or cuttings in late summer. Some species sucker freely; rooted suckers can be detached and grown on.

SWEET-PEA BUSH
Polygala
Fast growing, evergreen shrubs, flowering in spring and summer.

These shrubs have a natural tendency to legginess and dislike being cut back into bare wood to control it. Start pinching when the plants are young; after flowering, trim them lightly and then pinch the resulting new growth. Don't

try to rejuvenate old plants; discard and replace them. If you plant them in clumps rather than singly, they look much bushier.

Propagation Easy, by half-ripe cuttings in summer or seed sown in spring.

TAMARISK, flowering cypress
Tamarix
Deciduous shrubs, flowering in spring or summer.

The tamarisks fall into two groups: graceful, rather large shrubs that flower only in spring before the leaves appear and small trees that bloom in late spring or in summer, after the leaves. They aren't always properly labelled in nurseries, and you should let yours flower for a year or two to be certain which you have.

The spring flowerers, which include *T. tetrandra* and *T. juniperina*, flower on last summer's growth. They should be pruned sparingly after bloom, removing weak and twiggy branches. To limit their size, you can head back, but always to a strong lateral; and try not to cut too much or you'll turn what should be a graceful pink fountain into a dumpy untidiness. By removing the lower branches, you can make small trees of them. Also see the entry on Trees: Tamarisk.

Propagation Easy, by hardwood cuttings in winter or half-ripe cuttings in summer.

TEA TREE
Leptospermum
Fast growing, evergreen shrubs, flowering in spring and summer.

Never cut into bare wood, although tea trees will take light shearing (after bloom) and can be used as informal hedges. Normally, the only pruning needed is the removal of dead wood, which tends to

A tea tree can be converted to a small tree by removing the lower branches.

Tree peonies are soft-wooded shrubs— 'tree' is an overstatement.

clutter up the plants. The tallest species such as *L. laevigatum* and the lemon-scented *L. petersonii* can be trained as small, multi-stemmed trees by gradually removing the lowest of the branches.

Propagation Easy, from half-ripe cuttings in summer.

THYME
Thymus
Small, evergreen shrubs, some trailing, flowering in spring.

Grown as a culinary herb and for its sweetly fragrant leaves and flowers, the common thyme is a small soft-wooded shrub that may become straggly in a few years. It is neatest and most compact if it is trimmed back about halfway immediately after bloom. If you harvest sprigs lavishly (for drying) at flowering time, that will serve the same purpose. Treat the various fancy forms (woolly leaved, lemon scented and the rest) in the same way.

Propagation Easy, by seed sown in spring for the common thyme, by layering in summer for the fancy ones. You can take half-ripe cuttings in summer, too. The creeping thyme layers itself, and all you need to do is detach rooted pieces as you want them.

TREE PEONY
Paeonia suffruticosa and hybrids
Deciduous shrubs, flowering in spring months.

Tree peonies are an exception to the rule that spring-flowering shrubs are pruned after bloom. When the flowers fade, just snip them off, leaving the main pruning until early spring. Last year's growth will have died back a bit during the winter and will need to be headed back to the topmost vigorous-looking bud; but

The creeping thyme, Thymus serpyllum, *needs no trimming—but old plants are apt to die out in the middle and should be renewed by layering.*

don't cut any harder than that. Some authorities, however, claim that cutting a four- or five-year-old plant to the ground in late autumn or early winter (just once only!) will strengthen the roots and promote a bushier plant and more flowers. I haven't dared try it with my plant.

Propagation Slow and difficult—they are grafted in late winter onto pieces of herbaceous peony root, the intention being that the root keeps the tree peony scion alive until it can develop roots of its own, which may take two or three years. (This is why they are so expensive!) All types can readily be grown from fresh seed sown in autumn, although germination is slow, the plants may take up to seven years to flower and they are unlikely to come true.

TREE TOMATO, tamarillo
Cyphomandra betacea
Evergreen shrub, grown for its fruit.

Young plants should be pinched several times to make them bushy; established ones can be trimmed lightly after harvest or in early spring. They tend to become top-heavy and benefit from a stout stake. Plants are short lived; when they become straggly, it is best to replace them.

Propagation Easy, from seed sown in spring.

VERONICA
Hebe
Evergreen shrubs, flowering in spring and/or summer.

Most hebes are naturally shapely, bushy growers, needing little pruning but you can enhance the plants' natural bushiness and shapeliness by pinching young plants and heading back established ones

Even a close up like this shows the floppy habit of the tree tomato. To counteract it, the plants need post-harvest trimming and a stout stake.

lightly after bloom. An old bush that has become leggy can be hard pruned. Best time is early spring before growth begins; most species flower on the young wood.
Propagation Very easy, by softwood cuttings or layering in summer.

VIBURNUM
Viburnum
Evergreen or deciduous shrubs, flowering in spring.
The spring-flowering deciduous species can be treated in the same way as the snowball tree, but they are mostly slower growers and need attention only every few years. The evergreen species are mostly slow growing and shapely, and the only attention they should need is the heading back of the odd wayward branch. Also see Snowball tree.
Propagation Easy. The deciduous species can be grown from hardwood cuttings in autumn or softwood cuttings in late spring, the evergreens from half-ripe cuttings in late summer. All layer very readily in summer.

WARATAH
Telopea
Slow growing, evergreen shrubs, flowering in spring.
All the waratahs will grow leggy if you let them, but you can counteract the tendency, make them bushier and gain more flowers, by heading back after bloom. Or cut the flowers on long stems for the house.
Propagation Seed sown in spring may germinate but the plants need a symbiotic fungus on their roots to grow strongly—add a bit of soil from around the roots of the old plant to the potting mix to provide it. The new hybrids such as 'Shady Lady' and

'Braidwood Brilliant' are best grafted in spring on seedling stock, but they can be grown from half-ripe cuttings in summer. Don't expect a high percentage of strikes with these quite tricky natives.

WAX FLOWER
Eriostemon
Evergreen shrubs, flowering in spring months.
Naturally bushy and mounded in habit, eriostemons need little pruning other than the heading back of the occasional over-long branch, but you can trim them lightly after bloom to keep them compact. *E. myoporoides* can even be clipped into a simple topiary shape like a pyramid. Old and straggly plants can sometimes be rejuvenated by hard pruning after flowering, but don't count on it.
Propagation Fairly easy, from half-ripe cuttings or from layering in summer.

WEDDING BELLS
Deutzia
Deciduous shrubs, flowering in spring months.
Deutzias tend to start growing before the last flowers fade, and, although after bloom is the official pruning time, it is better to do it before the flowers are quite over. They make a thicket of stems and tend to fill themselves up with twiggy branches. Keep them tidy and full of flowers by cutting a couple of the oldest stems back to a strong shoot or to the ground each year. If you wish, you can also cut out the wood that has just flowered. It depends on just how tidy you want the plants.
Propagation Easy, by softwood cuttings taken in summer or by hardwood cuttings taken in late autumn.

WEIGELA
Weigela
Fast growing, deciduous shrubs, flowering in spring months.
Treat as wedding bells. Watch the variegated one for reversion, which it does very readily, and cut out all-green shoots as soon as you see them or they will take over. Despite their basically multi-stemmed habit, weigelas make handsome standards.
Propagation Easy, by hardwood cuttings in winter.

WINTERSWEET
Chimonanthus praecox
Deciduous shrub, flowering in winter and early spring.
Wintersweet makes a thicket of branches growing from ground level, and pruning normally consists of removing a couple of the oldest every other year or so. You can control the plant's size by heading back stems that have flowered, cutting to laterals or to fat buds. Alternatively, you can train the plant to a 3 m tall tree by removing the lowest branches. Prune immediately after bloom.
Propagation Fairly easy, by half-ripe cuttings or by layering in summer.

WORMWOOD, lad's love, absinthe
Artemisia
Evergreen, soft-wooded shrubs, flowering in summer.
Pinch young growth for bushiness; this may reduce flowering, but flowers aren't much to look at anyway. Old plants are apt to become straggly but can be brought back to good form by heading back halfway in winter or early spring. Remove spent flowers for neatness.
Propagation Easy, from cuttings of the young growth in spring and summer. Most types layer easily.

This is the new hybrid waratah 'Shady Lady', bushier in habit and easier to propagate than its parent, Telopea speciosissima, *but like it benefiting from a light post-flowering trim.*

Weigela's bare stalks can look most unappealing in winter—but resist the temptation to prune them or there will be no flowers. Wait until after bloom.

Wormwood—also known as lad's love or maid's ruin—is a floppy bush, much quieter in appearance than its reputation suggests.

YELLOW ELDER

Tecoma stans, formerly *Stenolobium stans*

Fast growing, evergreen shrub, flowering in summer or most of the year in sub-tropical climates. The yellow elder is much improved by heading back about halfway in spring and thinning out some of the oldest branches every couple of years. Removing spent flowers helps bring on more. An old, leggy plant can be renewed by hard pruning in early spring.

Propagation Easy, from half-ripe cuttings in summer.

YELLOW OLEANDER

Thevetia

Fast growing, evergreen shrubs, flowering in summer.

The yellow oleander is a large shrub that can be trained into a small tree by removing lower branches or sheared as a 2.5 m tall hedge, but looks well without any pruning. If you want to bring a tall plant down to size, cut hard in spring, and with pinching and selective heading back and thinning you can hold it to 1.5 m. Wear gloves and eye protection, as the sticky sap is poisonous.

Propagation Very easy, by layering or half-ripe cuttings taken in summer.

ZEBRA PLANT

Aphelandra

Fast growing, evergreen shrubs, flowering in summer.

Usually grown as indoor plants, they will do quite well in frost-free gardens. Indoors or out, prune for bushiness in early spring, heading back about halfway and removing weak branches, but don't cut into old wood. Remove spent flowers to encourage bloom.

Propagation Fairly easy, from cuttings of non-flowering shoots in summer.

TREES

Trees are the longest lived plants in the garden, so choose them with care and match to the space you have available. Before you plant, see a mature specimen—there is no better way of assessing if the species is right for you and it will help when you are training and pruning. Pruning a tree can be a big job but happily it isn't a frequent one, and it calls not so much for skill as for artistry.

ALDER
Alnus

Fast growing, deciduous or evergreen trees, flowering in spring.

Young trees can be trained as single- or multi-stemmed trees; they tend to branch low and may need their crowns raised. Mature trees need only the removal (in winter) of crossing or dead branches. Suckers from the base may compete with the main tree and should be removed.

Propagation Easy from seed sown in spring; they can be grown with more difficulty from winter cuttings.

ALMOND
Prunus dulcis

Fairly fast growing, deciduous trees, flowering in spring and grown for their fruit.

Young trees should be given an initial pruning to develop a good shape. Established trees are pruned to ensure a constant supply of new wood that bears the flowers and fruit. Fruiting spurs bear for about five years—each winter remove about a fifth of the oldest. If a young tree reacts to pruning by producing masses of non-fruiting growth, stop pruning for a year or two until it settles down. Remove weak and crossing branches as you notice them. The flowering almond (*P.* 'Pollardii') needs no regular pruning, although it tends to branch low and benefits from early training to gain a reasonable length of trunk. Almonds are self-sterile; you need two trees of different varieties to get fruit. This is not necessary with the flowering almond, as its fruit is inferior anyway.

Propagation Moderately easy, by budding on almond or peach seedlings.

APPLE
Malus cultivars

Fairly fast growing, deciduous trees, flowering in spring.

An unpruned apple will bear much fruit as long as it has another tree of a different variety nearby to pollinate it but it is likely to be inconveniently large, with most of the fruit on the difficult-to-reach upper branches. Pruning makes a tree of manageable size, roughly pyramidal or vase shaped, so that all the branches can get the sun and thus bear fruit within reach. Give the young tree the usual initial training to establish a framework of four or five well-spaced branches. You may have to cut the tree hard at planting time to induce it to branch. Cut out unwanted branches in winter, taking out horizontal ones to make the tree grow taller, vertical ones to make it wider. It may take four or five years to come into bearing, and then the main pruning season shifts to summer. Now you don't want long shoots to increase the tree's size, but plenty of the short spurs that bear flowers and fruit for several years. Head back the long shoots that arise after flowering to three or four leaves once growth has stopped. They will make spur-growth either at once or in spring. (If you leave them unpruned, they will probably make most of their spurs near the base anyway.)

To extend the size of the tree or fill in any gaps in the crown, let appropriate shoots grow long. Remember, for

Apple blossoms grow on short spurs that continue to flower for several years. Pruning seeks to encourage the maximum number of these on a compact tree.

Before

After

Thinning fruit results in larger fruit, and it can correct biennial bearing.

growth, prune in winter; for flowers and fruit, prune in summer only.

Apples have a bad habit of biennial bearing: a bumper crop one year, few or no flowers next year. To remedy this, thin out the young fruit drastically in an 'on' year. When they are about a quarter full grown, pick off half or even 60 per cent of them, leaving the remainder evenly spaced along the branches. They will grow much bigger than if you hadn't thinned, and the weight of crop won't be significantly reduced. As with all grafted trees, watch out for suckers from the rootstock and pull them off. The foliage won't be much different from the scion variety, but that shouldn't matter—treat any shoot that arises below your lowest main branch as a sucker.

Propagation Moderately easy, by budding in late spring. The rootstocks are usually grown from root cuttings taken in winter, and there are several strains in use, designed to give larger or smaller trees. Seedlings may occasionally come up if you threw an apple core on the compost heap, but it will be some years before you know if the tree has taken true to type.

APPLE BOX
Angophora
Evergreen trees, flowering in summer.

These are related to *Eucalyptus* and treated in the same way. *A. costata* and *A. intermedia* need no pruning other than occasional removal of dead wood; *A. cordifolia* is a mallee-like shrub. Control its size by removing selected branches down to the base.
Propagation Easy, from fresh seed sown in spring.

These old apple trees, at Riversdale, Goulburn, NSW, were originally trained espalier on the fence, but are now growing more or less freely and bearing well.

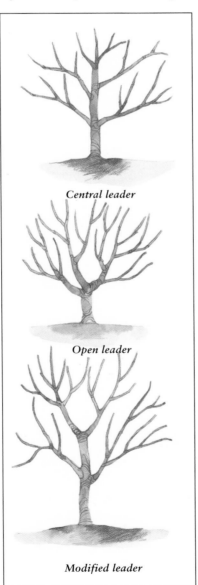

Central leader

Open leader

Modified leader

Three systems for training an apple tree. A central leader is strongest.

Young tree: cut off weak and crowded branches.

Dwarf tree: cut long and weak branches.

Mature tree: cut overly vigorous and weak branches.

Pruning apple trees. Always remove any weak or crossing branches.

In this formal garden at Kennerton Green, Mittagong, NSW, bay trees are clipped as standards, each with a circle of box around its feet.

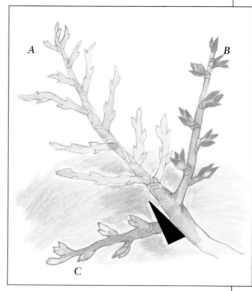

Pruning an apricot tree. Each year remove branches (C) that are three or four years old. Branch B is new. Branch A will be pruned next year.

Creating a standard bay tree. 1 Select a plant with a prominent stem and when it has reached the height you want, cut off the growing tip. Remove any side branches that are below the base of the head and trim back the other branches to two or three leaves. 2 At the end of the following summer, cut off the leader to encourage new side branches. 3 At the beginning and end of each summer pinch out the growing tips to maintain the rounded head.

APRICOT
Prunus armeniaca
Fast growing, deciduous trees, flowering in spring.
The apricot is a spur bearer like the apple and the general rules for pruning are similar. However, the spurs remain productive only for three or four years and so you need to prune more in order to have more new growth. After the initial training to shape, there won't be much to do for a few years; then you will want to cut out the oldest branches to strong young ones and thin last year's growth a little to ensure the tree doesn't waste its energy in too much fruit. Do this in winter; in summer, let the tree grow as it pleases. Thin the fruit sufficiently to ensure the ripening fruits don't rub against each other, as any injury makes them susceptible to brown rot.

The Japanese apricot (*P. mume* and its varieties) is treated much more simply than the fruiting types. Young trees need the usual training but then need little pruning other than occasional thinning out of overcrowded growth. The best time is early in the flowering period or immediately after bloom, but it can be done in winter. The trees are sometimes pollarded after bloom to encourage long spikes of flowers, but this is entirely optional.
Propagation Moderately easy, by budding in late spring on seedling stock. Apricot, plum or peach seedlings can be used, and each has its admirers.

ASH
Fraxinus
Deciduous trees.
Young ashes tend to form weak, V-shaped crotches and need care in training—allow only those branches growing out wide from the trunk to develop. Mature trees need little pruning other than removal of dead wood. They tend to cast rather heavy shade, which can be lightened by thinning out weaker branches.
Propagation Easy, by autumn-sown seed; selected forms such as the golden and claret ashes are budded on seedling stock in summer. Watch out for suckers from the stock on young trees.

AUSTRALIAN CYPRESS,
cypress pine
Callitris
Evergreen coniferous trees, random branching.
The several species are all naturally compact and shapely, and they don't need pruning. Although not commonly used for the purpose, they make good tall hedges; shear as needed, but don't cut into any old wood.
Propagation Fairly easy, from seed in spring or summer, or from cuttings, inserted in sandy soil in summer.

AVOCADO
Persea americana
Evergreen fruit tree, flowering in summer months.
Young trees can be given the usual training, but normally they develop perfectly well without it. Inside branches on mature trees are inclined to die off naturally; remove them for neatness. No other pruning is needed, but you can control the size of the tree by gentle heading back immediately after harvest. Don't ever cut away enough foliage to expose the trunk and limbs to the sun; the bark is very easily sunburnt.
Propagation Fairly easy, by grafting named varieties onto seedling stock. Avocado seeds germinate very easily, but seedlings are most unreliable.

BANANA
Musa species and varieties
Fast growing, giant herbaceous plants, flowering at almost any time.
Despite its palm-like appearance, the banana is a herbaceous plant; after the fruit ripens, the 'tree' dies, to be replaced by new shoots from the rootstock. Commercial growers cut the whole thing down at harvest, and that is the simplest way in the garden also. Ornamental species look best if dead leaves are regularly removed; if they flower, the flowers can be allowed to remain until the plant begins to die off, when it can be cut to the ground and fertilised to encourage the offshoots. Wear stout rubber gloves and old clothes when pruning; the sap will stain your hands (and your clothes) black.
Propagation Easy, by removing rooted suckers before they are too large to handle.

BAY TREE, laurel
Laurus nobilis
Slow growing, evergreen tree, grown for the flavour its leaves add to cooking. Summer flowers are unimportant.
It is naturally a shapely, multi-stemmed tree and doesn't need pruning, but the bay tree can take hard cutting and shearing, and it is often used for hedging and topiary—standard bays, their heads clipped into spheres, are a tradition in France. To shape a topiary bay, remove any unwanted branches in late winter and clip as needed through the summer. Unpruned bays branch low, and as the tree develops you may want to remove the lower branches to reveal the trunks.
Propagation Not very easy. Autumn-sown seed is easiest;

half-ripe cuttings in summer will root slowly, but layering or air-layering is a better bet.

BEECH
Fagus
Slow growing, deciduous tree.
Once established beeches need little pruning, other than the gradual removal of lower branches as the tree develops. They will take hard pruning and regular clipping, and can be used to make tall hedges.
Propagation Fairly easy, from seed sown in autumn. Selected forms such as the copper and tricoloured beeches are usually budded in late summer on seedling stock.

BIRCH
Betula
Fast growing, deciduous tree.
The general rule with birches is to prune as little as possible; they don't grow back well. If a young tree develops two leaders, cut the weaker out in winter—they usually form a weak crotch and the tree can be torn apart in a storm. Weak branches can be cut right out. To achieve a multi-trunked tree, plant two or three seedlings together; it is possible to cut a young tree down and have it regrow several stems, but don't count on it. It can be tempting to peel the curling bark from the trunk to reveal the glossy new bark beneath, but the artificially revealed bark will die and leave ugly scars.
Propagation Easy, by sowing fresh seed in spring; just press it into the compost without covering it. Don't expect all to germinate; even fresh seed has fairly low fertility. Fancy varieties such as cut leaved and weeping birches are grafted with moderate difficulty on seedlings of the same species.

BLACK LOCUST, FALSE ACACIA
Robinia
Fast growing, deciduous trees and shrubs, flowering in spring. Most often seen are *R. pseudo-acacia* and its varieties, such as the yellow-leaved 'Frisia' and 'Decaisneana', the so-called pink wisteria tree. They need careful training in youth, as they are inclined to develop weak crotches and long, straggly branches. Cut out branches that aren't growing out at wide angles from the main stem and shorten any stragglers as needed. Once the framework is established, the trees need little pruning, which is just as well as large wounds don't heal well and are prone to rot. If you do need to cut out a broken or misplaced branch, cut to a lateral or the main trunk. Winter is the best pruning time. Suckers are likely to be a problem—pull them out as soon as you see them. *R. hispida* is a suckering shrub. You may need to remove suckers from time to time to keep the plant where you want it; otherwise, all it needs is occasional cutting out of one or two of the oldest, least productive branches in winter.
Propagation Very easy, from seed sown in autumn, although most of the seedlings will be viciously thorny. *R. hispida* is easy from hardwood cuttings or by detaching suckers in winter; the selected forms of *R. pseudoacacia* are budded in spring on seedling rootstock, which is notoriously prone to producing thorny suckers.

BLEEDING HEART,
Queensland poplar
Omalanthus populifolius
Fast growing, evergreen small tree.
This overgrown shrub or small tree gets its name from its heart-shaped leaves, a few of which are usually about to fall and turning red. It can be trained to one or several stems (head the young plant back to force multiple stems) and can have the lower branches removed as it matures. It is inclined to get top-heavy and benefits from thinning at any time, cutting excess branches back to strong laterals and removing dead wood.
Propagation Very easy, from spring-sown seed; a little less easy from half-ripe cuttings in late summer.

BLUEBERRY ASH
Elaeocarpus reticulatus
Evergreen tree, flowering in spring months.
Naturally elegant in habit, the blueberry ash needs little pruning. It tends to branch low, and you can raise the crown by removing the lower branches. Best times are in winter or in autumn when growth has settled down. Dead wood can be removed at any time.
Propagation Easy, from half-ripe cuttings in summer. Seed germinates freely in spring, but don't expect all seedlings from the pink form to come pink.

BUNYA PINE
Araucaria bidwillii
Large coniferous evergreen tree.
Naturally shapely, this doesn't need pruning. Young trees sometimes develop double leaders; cut out the weaker of the two in winter. Make any cuts back to another branch.
Propagation Fairly easy, by seed in summer.

CAMPHOR LAUREL
Cinnamomum camphora
Fast growing, evergreen tree.
The camphor laurel can be pollarded, but it really needs no regular pruning. Every few

years you can thin the crown, taking out dead branches and dense growth, to get more sun through. This massive tree has greedy roots and belongs only in the biggest gardens.

Propagation Easy, from seed in spring or cuttings of half-ripe growth in summer. Easier still, wait for self-sown seedlings to come up around a mature tree and transplant them in autumn.

CAPE CHESTNUT
Calodendrum capense
Evergreen tree, flowering in summer months.

You can remove the lower branches of young trees to encourage them to branch high, but they don't really need it, and established trees need no regular pruning. You can let more light through to the garden by thinning out some of the weaker branches, taking them back to another limb or right to the trunk.

Propagation Fairly easy, from seed sown in spring, although seedlings can take a long time to flower; it is better to graft from an established, profuse-blooming tree onto seedling stock of this plant.

CAPE LEEUWIN WATTLE,
tree-in-a-hurry
Albizia lophantha
Fast growing, evergreen tree, flowering in summer.

Before you plant this tree, check whether you are allowed to grow it in your area. It is exceptionally fast growing and, like its cousins the wattles, not very long lived. Also like them, it fills up its crown with dead branches; prune to remove these. Older trees are liable to attack by borers and should be removed, not left to die.

Propagation Easy, from seed sown in spring.

This young beech is offset by a neatly trimmed sasanqua camellia.

This bunya pine shows the result of not nipping a double leader in the bud.

Admired for its lavish summer bloom, the cape chestnut is a fine shade tree for mild winter climates. It grows fairly slowly.

The only pruning a cedar needs is to have straggly over-long branches cut back to a top-facing shoot.

Most cassias seed abundantly; to forestall crops of seedlings all over the garden, give them a post-flowering trim.

This is the weeping form of Prunus subhirtella, *most popular of weeping cherries. They are usually budded on tall standards, but you can train a tree from the ground up if you start young. Simply tie the leading shoot to a tall, stout stake and wait.*

CAROB

Ceratonia siliqua

Evergreen tree or oversize shrub, flowering in spring.

The carob, a giant shrub branching to the ground and with several trunks, can be trained as a single-stemmed tree but looks best multi-stemmed. It takes heavy pruning and clipping and can be used as a tall hedge, but clipping will reduce the yield of the chocolate-like pods. Best time for major pruning is winter.

Propagation Easy, if a trifle slow, from seed sown as soon as it is ripe in autumn.

CASSIA

Cassia

Evergreen or partly deciduous trees and shrubs, flowering in summer or autumn.

C. bicapsularis and the very similar *C. corymbosa*, commonly grown for their gold flowers in autumn, benefit from trimming away the spent flower clusters after bloom to discourage fruiting (and cassia seedlings) and keep the plant compact. This will hold them as large shrubs; to train them as trees, remove lower branches in autumn. Take out dead wood to keep the trees presentable. They are not long lived. Small, shrubby types need only to have spent flower clusters removed. Don't cut into old wood, as it won't shoot. Also see Indian laburnum, Pink shower.

Propagation Easy, from fresh seed sown in spring. Soak it first, before planting.

CEDAR

Cedrus

Evergreen, coniferous trees.

Cedars need no regular pruning, but if they are branching too low, raise the crown by removing a few of the lowest branches in winter. Don't do it all at once; spread the job over two or three years. Young trees sometimes send out one or two horizontal branches longer than the others, making them look lop-sided. These can be cut back to a suitable lateral, but be patient; they will grow out of awkward adolescence quite soon.

Propagation Easy, from seed sown as soon as it is ripe and the cones begin to break up in autumn. Fancy varieties such as the weeping form of *C. atlantica* or the golden *C. deodara* don't usually come true from seed and are best grafted onto seedlings in autumn, a skilled operation.

CHERRY

Prunus

Fast growing, deciduous trees, flowering in spring.

Cherries heal their wounds only slowly, and so prune as little as possible. Young fruiting cherries (*P. avium*) may need weak or badly placed branches removed, but established trees will only need occasional thinning out of weak twigs that crowd the tree's centre. Do any pruning that is necessary in winter, soon after leaf fall.

The flowering cherries (*P. serrulata*) are treated much more simply. Young trees need the usual training to ensure a strong stem and well-spaced branches. Some are apt to grow like blown-out umbrellas and you may need to prune regularly in the tree's youth to establish a graceful habit, cutting back to horizontal branches or to outward facing buds. Later they need little pruning other than occasional thinning out of overcrowded growth. The best time for this is early in the flowering period or immediately after bloom; but you can also prune in winter. If you want to improve the shape of a cherry tree (some varieties are not very graceful), cut awkwardly placed branches back to laterals in late summer, when the wounds will heal better than in winter. *P. glandulosa*, the dwarf or bush cherry, is traditionally cut back hard each year immediately after bloom, to encourage long wands of flowers to arise straight from the ground; but it can be left to grow as a mounding, metre-tall shrub; simply remove a couple of the oldest, twiggiest branches every couple of years.

The cherry laurels, *P. laurocerasus* and *P. lusitanica*, are large evergreen shrubs that can be allowed to grow unpruned or trained as small trees by progressively removing the lower branches as the plants mature; but they are most often planted as hedges, when they can be clipped formally after bloom. (Use secateurs as shears will cut the leaves in half.) They will grow back from bare wood, and so an overgrown hedge can be dealt with severely. Winter is the best time for this, despite the loss of a season's flowers. They aren't so very exciting anyway.

Propagation Moderately easy, by budding in late summer onto seedling understocks. You can try hardwood cuttings in winter, but don't expect a high percentage of strikes. Some ornamental cherries can be grown from seed sown in autumn but they are best struck from hardwood or root cuttings in winter. The Japanese cherries are best budded in early summer onto seedling understocks. The weeping cherries are almost always budded as standards on stems 2 m tall.

CHESTNUT
Castanea sativa
Slow growing, deciduous tree, flowering in spring.
Young trees can be given the usual training; established trees need little pruning other than removal of dead wood.
Propagation Fresh seed sown in autumn germinates easily. Budded trees, selected for early and profuse bearing, are sometimes available and are to be preferred to seedlings.

CHINESE TALLOW TREE
Sapium sebiferum
Fairly fast growing, deciduous tree, flowering insignificantly in spring; superb autumn foliage.
Naturally rather shrubby with a tendency to multiple trunks, the tallow tree needs careful training if you want to grow it on a tall, single stem. It tends to make its shoots in whorls, and it isn't always clear which is going to become the leader. Stake the most likely and pinch back the others. Alternatively, give the tree its head for a couple of years, then remove any too-low branches in winter. Established trees need no pruning other than removal of dead branches and maybe a gentle shaping in winter. The tips of last year's growths die back in winter, but the resulting small dead twigs will be hidden by new foliage and will soon break off.
Propagation Easy, by seed in spring or half-ripe cuttings in summer. Select seedlings carefully: those with red-tinted young growth usually have the richest autumn colour.

CITRUS
Citrus and *Fortunella*
Evergreen trees or shrubs, grown for their fruit.
Citrus trees include orange (C. *sinensis*), lemon (C. *limon*),

mandarin (C. *reticulata*), grapefruit (C. *paradisi*) and cumquat *(Fortunella)*. The rule is that you don't prune citrus, you feed them, but they will take hard pruning if they have to. Normally all that is needed is to remove dead or spindly, twiggy wood. As the trees develop, they will shed lower branches naturally, and you can hasten the process by removing any that are being shaded out. If you want to walk under the trees, lower branches can be removed: usually this won't affect the crop, but lemons tend to bear a lot of fruit on branches weeping down almost to the ground. Overcrowded branches can be removed, but don't open the crown up too much by thinning or you will expose the bark to the risk of sunburn.

Overgrown, neglected trees are best dealt with by removing all dead branches back to sound wood; if that leaves a straggling skeleton, you can cut the main branches hard, but you will then need to protect the bark from sunburn; paint them with a water based paint—the sort used to shade the glass on greenhouses is the best. If the tree is basically healthy, there will be so much growth you'll have to thin it. But don't expect fruit for a couple of years.

Container grown trees can have their size controlled by heading back the young growth and by pruning the roots every couple of years—it was to facilitate this operation that the traditional 'Versailles tub' with its removable bottom was developed.
Propagation Fairly easy, by budding on rootstock in summer, but it is extremely difficult for home gardeners to obtain suitable rootstocks. All

grow easily from seed, with a better than usual chance of reasonable results.

CORAL TREE
Erythrina
Deciduous trees, flowering at various times of the year.
The big species such as *E. variegata (E. indica)*, the Indian coral tree and the South African *E. caffra* need no regular pruning other than the removal of dead or broken branches, but they are shallow rooted and benefit from thinning to decrease their wind resistance—a big job on an established tree. They can be pruned in winter, cutting right back to another branch as stumps rot very easily. The flowering shoots of *E. cristagalli* die back a little after bloom, and it is often cut back hard at that time, a treatment that keeps it as a large shrub. If grown as a tree, it will need annual clearing out of dead wood to keep it presentable.
Propagation Very easy, from cuttings in spring. Quite large branches of *E. indica* will root if they are kept moist.

CRAB-APPLE
Malus
Deciduous trees, flowering in spring months.
Crab-apples are naturally dense and twiggy. They can be left unpruned but will look more elegant if given early training to establish a framework of well-spaced branches. To open up the crowns of established trees, remove any branches that are going to cross over the tree's centre and thin too dense branches. Prune in winter or after flowering, as you like. It's easier to see what you're doing in winter, but the tree will respond with new growth that you may not

You can see how many branches need-ed removal to train this young Chinese tallow tree to a single stem.

Growing citrus in pots is an old tradition. They flourish best if their roots are pruned every few years—tip them out, shave a centimetre or two off the root ball and replant.

New shoots will grow here.

Citrus rarely need pruning but you can cut back the fruiting shoots to encour-age fruit closer to the centre of the tree.

You can remove some of the lower branches of a lemon tree to allow other plants to grow beneath it, but don't overdo it. This tree is kept flourishing by an annual fertilising and regular cleaning out of dead wood. The variety is 'Eureka'.

Look carefully at the elm on the right, and you can see where a large low branch has been removed and has healed perfectly. Elms sucker strongly if the roots are disturbed; a position in grass like this suits them best.

Crab-apples lend themselves to espalier just as fruiting apples do, but it is not usual to train them quite so formally as here, at Charleton, Goulburn, NSW. This is 'Purpurea', with deep pink flowers and dark leaves. It fruits rather sparingly; grow it for the flowers.

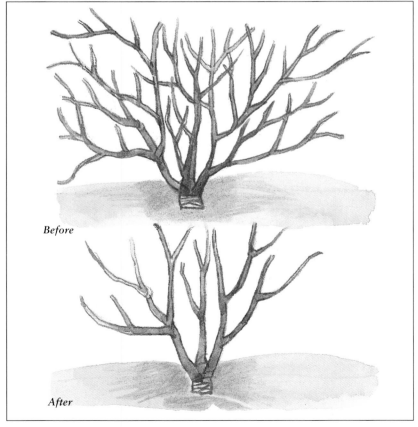

Before

After

To produce a well-shaped crab-apple, prune regularly to remove tangled, twiggy growth. After pruning watch for new, unwanted shoots.

want—rub off any unwanted shoots. There will be less new growth from early summer pruning, but it's not so easy to see what you are doing. If you want crab-apples for jelly, prune the tree the way you would a regular apple, but usually the crop will be big enough without going to that amount of trouble. Like regular apples, crab-apples can be trained as espaliers.

Propagation Easy, by root cuttings in winter, although nurseries often bud selected varieties on seedling stock in late spring. This means you need to take care if you are striking a root cutting; you don't want to find you are propagating an understock. Keep a close watch for alien foliage.

CUSTARD APPLE, cherimoya
Annona
Semi-deciduous small tree, flowering in summer.

Young custard apples need only routine removal of badly placed branches to ensure a good framework; established trees can be left unpruned, but they branch very low and you may want to remove the lowest branches to raise the crown. Otherwise, simply remove dead and overcrowded wood. The tree is unusual in that growth buds will not develop until the adjacent leaf is removed; you can, by strategically removing leaves, encourage the tree to grow just where you want it. The tree can be trained as an informal espalier. Prune when the tree is in leaf-shedding mode; it is not completely deciduous.

Propagation Moderately easy, by grafting on seedling stock. 'African Pride', sometimes used as an understock, can be propagated from cuttings taken in summer months.

CYPRESS, pencil pine
Cupressus
Evergreen, coniferous trees, random branching.

The Italian cypress or pencil pine (*C. sempervirens*) has a narrow, columnar habit, but some trees allow odd branches to arch outwards, often under the weight of a heavy crop of cones. Don't try to bundle everything up with wire—it is better to cut off the errant branch to a lateral just below the point where it pulls away. Growth from other branches will soon fill up the gap. Don't cut the leader to control the height; you will end up with a most inelegant, flat-topped tree. Other species, such as the Monterey cypress (*C. macrocarpa*), *C. torulosa* and *C. arizonica*, are densely pyramidal when young, becoming wider and more open with maturity. Then you can enhance their form by raising the crown, cleaning out dead wood (there will be lots under the outer foliage) and judiciously thinning weaker branches. Otherwise, cypresses need no regular pruning. You can prune, if desired, at almost any time.

Cypresses can be sheared as formal hedges, but they are big trees and trying to keep them lower than about 2.5 m is constant work. Don't cut into bare wood, as it won't regrow.

Propagation Easy, from seed sown in spring. Cuttings taken in late summer root fairly readily and are the best way to propagate selected forms such as 'Swanes Golden'.

DAWN REDWOOD
Metasequoia glyptostroboides
Fast growing, deciduous conifer, random branching.

The dawn redwood is shapely by nature and needs no pruning, but you can selectively

head back the side branches to create a narrower column of foliage. Don't cut the leader, and remember that this is a fairly tall tree—as it matures you'll need a very long ladder! The natural habit is to branch right to the ground, but you can remove some of the lower branches from a mature tree to allow you to walk under it.

Propagation Quite easy, from seed in autumn or half-ripe cuttings or layering in summer.

DOGWOOD
Cornus
Evergreen or deciduous trees, flowering in spring.

The deciduous pink or white flowering American dogwood should be pruned as little as possible, as it heals its wounds very slowly—confine yourself to removing dead wood. If you have to take off a broken branch, always cut back to another branch or the trunk. The same applies to the evergreen *C. capitata* and *C. chinensis*, which are more shrubby in their growth. If you want to train them as trees (they look best multi-trunked), remove the lower branches early, while they are still small.

Propagation Moderately easy, by softwood cuttings or layering in summer.

ELM
Ulmus
Fast growing, deciduous or evergreen trees, flowering in winter or spring, although flowers are unimportant.

The deciduous elms (*U. procera, U. americana, U. glabra* and the golden elm, 'Louis Van Houtte') need only the usual young-tree training to ensure they grow tall and straight. Once they begin to mature, no pruning is needed other than removal of dead wood. If you

Many of the smaller eucalypts, such as these at Everglades, Leura, NSW, although not strictly mallees, branch low and develop picturesque, informal shapes.

Densely branched right to the ground in youth, the false cypresses lose their lower branches with maturity. You can assist the process when the trees are grown.

need to remove a misplaced branch, do it in winter or in late summer, cutting back to a lateral; stubs will respond with a bunch of twiggy shoots. The evergreen or almost evergreen Chinese elm, *U. parvifolia*, needs more care in its youth. The young branches are very limber and tend to droop, and you need to stake the young tree carefully and ensure that it doesn't branch too low. Over-long branches may need heading back to an upward-growing lateral. All elms sucker freely, especially if the roots are cut. Pull suckers out when you see them.

Propagation Easy, by detaching suckers in autumn, taking cuttings in summer or sowing seed in autumn. The golden elm and other named varieties are usually budded in summer on seedling stock.

EUCALYPTUS
Eucalyptus
Fast growing, evergreen trees, flowering at various times throughout the year.
Eucalypts will grow back vigorously from heavy pruning but it can be dangerous to subject them to it—the new branches are never very securely attached and can tear off at the base, often years later. If a tree really is too big for its position, consider replacing it with a smaller one. Normally all the pruning needed is removal of dead wood and the occasional removal of a branch that is getting in the way or spoiling the shape of the tree, both of which you can do at any time. (Make all cuts back to another branch or to the trunk.) Old eucalypts are often hollow and provide nesting places for native birds and animals; take a tree surgeon's advice before deciding such a

tree is dangerous. If a tree is badly defoliated by insects or burnt in a bushfire, wait a year to see how it recovers before doing any remedial pruning.

Young trees rarely need training—they will settle the arrangement of their branches for themselves as they mature, and any crookedness in the trunk will even out. Don't stake them or their roots will be weak; if a young tree becomes top-heavy and falls over, bend its top to the ground and fix it there with a short stake. It will send up one or several strong shoots from the base; in a year or so you can remove all but the strongest of the shoots.

Most of the commonly grown forest eucalypts are naturally single trunked, and to make a clump it is simplest to plant several close together. Many of the smaller species are mallees, which normally make clumps of more or less evenly sized stems growing from a massive rootstock called a lignotuber. If you are faced with a leggy mallee, you can cut it to the ground in late winter, thus forcing it to make new trunks, and then thinning out the weakest. *E. erythrocorys*, although not strictly a mallee, often becomes straggly after ten years or so and can be rejuvenated by this treatment. The shrubby types such as *E. tetragona* can be treated similarly if they become over-large, but actually they need little pruning other than removal of dead wood—if one gets a bit thin, encourage new growth with water and fertiliser. Some mallee species such as *E. lehmannii* can be trained as single- or multi-stemmed trees as you wish.
Propagation Easy, by spring- or autumn-sown seed. Be sure

to transplant the young trees to their final positions while they are small; if they become pot-bound, their roots can be reluctant to break out into the surrounding soil and give the tree firm support. Outside the laboratory there has so far been little success in propagating eucalypts vegetatively: cuttings and layerings consistently refuse to root, and grafting has proved very difficult.

FALSE ARALIA
Dizygotheca elegantissima
Fast growing, evergreen tree, often grown as an indoor plant.
The lacy leaves that look so charming on indoor plants are the juvenile form of the foliage; when the tree is planted out in frost-free gardens, it eventually develops much coarser (but still handsome) adult leaves. Cut it back hard in spring, and the new growth will return to the juvenile state, at least for a while. The tree is always multi-stemmed and upright, and you can have foliage at various levels by cutting the stems back to various heights; it will grow back wherever you cut it.
Propagation Cuttings made from leafless sections of stem will root quite easily in summer; indoor plants can also be air-layered.

FALSE CYPRESS
Chamaecyparis
Evergreen, coniferous trees; random branching.
While most of the species are large trees, there are many dwarf cultivars grown in rock gardens. All are symmetrical and dense in growth (at least while young) and rarely need pruning. They can be held to size by pinching the new growth and occasional thinning, but it is not easy to keep

them looking natural for long under this treatment. They take shearing well and are sometimes used for large (2 m or more) formal hedges or for topiary—but take care not to cut beyond the foliage as bare wood rarely sprouts.
Propagation Fairly easy, from cuttings in summer. They root slowly, and rooting hormone is a great help.

FIDDLEWOOD
Citharexylum spinosum
Evergreen tree, flowering in summer months.
Naturally low branching, the fiddlewood can be grown as an outsize shrub or a tree by removing the lower branches as it matures. With early training, you can train it on a single stem. (The branches tend to uprightness, and a multi-stemmed tree will usually have a broader, better balanced crown.) No regular pruning is needed, but the plant can take hard pruning and can be sheared as a formal hedge.
Propagation Fairly easy, by half-ripe cuttings taken in late spring.

FIG, ornamental fig, rubber tree
Ficus
Fast growing, evergreen or deciduous trees and climbers.
The big evergreen trees such as *F. hillii* and the Moreton Bay fig (*F. macrophylla*) can be pruned hard (at any time during warm weather) if need be, but they are far too big for most gardens; think twice before planting them. That goes for the rubber trees (*F. elastica* and *F. lyrata*) too; if the office pot plant gets too big, don't plant it in the garden. However, if there is room for them in your garden, they need no pruning other than

You can still take cuttings of frangipanis in summer when the trees are in bloom, but don't be surprised if the leaves fall off. New ones will grow once roots are made.

This golden chain tree is 'Vossii'. Like all laburnums, it's best in a cool climate.

Grown in the open like this, firs naturally retain their lowest branches.

Prune the fruiting fig in winter. Thin out weak branches and remove suckers.

removal of dead branches. *F. hillii* can be clipped as a tall hedge or for large-scale topiary, but be wary of its greedy roots. It is sometimes trained as a standard, clipping the crown into a sphere, and can be kept in a large tub if you tip it out and prune the roots occasionally. *F. pumila* is a rampant, self-clinging vine, quite capable of covering a five-storey building. To control its size, it can be pruned ruthlessly, even cutting it to the ground, in spring or summer, with out-of-bounds shoots removed at any time. It eventually develops coarse adult foliage, but regular clipping will ensure a supply of the daintier juvenile leaves, pink when young, that are indeed its chief attraction.

The fruiting fig (*F. carica*) is a deciduous shrubby tree that bears two crops, one in early summer on last year's wood, and then a second in late summer on shoots that grew while the first crop was ripening. Pruning aims to keep the tree compact and encourage a constant supply of new wood. Let young trees grow as they please in the first summer and then in the first winter remove any shoots growing upright in the centre, to ensure that you get your main branches low down where picking is easier. Aim for a vase shaped tree, but don't let it be too open in the centre; you need foliage to shade the trunk and main limbs against sunburn. Once the framework is established, in about three years, each winter cut out any weak or crowded growth and head back the outer branches if necessary to control the size. You may need to head back young growth in summer a little for the same reason, but try to keep summer pruning to a minimum as it reduces the second crop. Figs are often grown as espaliers, but they do not make as elegant a form as apples and the summer pruning required limits the crop. Old, straggly and unproductive trees can be renewed by drastic pruning in winter, followed by some thinning of new growth; don't expect much of a crop for a couple of years.

Propagation Easy, by half-ripe cuttings in summer or by air-layering. Figs are among the easiest plants to air layer, and this gives the best way to deal with that too-big rubber tree. Air-layer the top half metre or so to provide a compact new plant and discard the old one.

The fruiting fig is best propagated by hardwood cuttings in winter. To save transplanting shock, put them one to a pot.

FIR
Abies
Coniferous, evergreen trees, whorl branching.
No pruning is needed other than removal of dead or damaged branches, cutting back to an undamaged branch or right back to the trunk. Don't try to control size by pruning; you'll only ruin the plant's shape.
Propagation Quite easy, from seed in spring or autumn.

FIREWHEEL TREE
Stenocarpus sinuatus
Fairly slow growing, evergreen tree, flowering in summer.
Young trees can be rather gawky and stiff; you can head back any branches that are spoiling the shape, but it isn't really necessary as the tree usually grows out of it. Mature trees need no pruning.
Propagation Easy, by seed sown in spring; fairly easy, by half-ripe cuttings in summer.

FRANGIPANI
Plumeria
Fast growing, evergreen or deciduous trees, flowering in summer.
Frangipanis need little pruning but you might occasionally need to shorten an out-of-balance branch or two to a strong lateral, or trim off lower branches to raise the crown. Prune at almost any time in warm climates; in temperate areas the best time is in spring, after the weather has warmed up but before growth begins. You can control size by selective heading back and thinning, but this is constant work.
Propagation Very easy, from cuttings taken late winter to early spring; quite large branches will take root, giving instant trees. Leave the cuttings out of the ground for a few days to allow the milky sap to congeal before inserting them.

GOLDEN CHAIN TREE
Laburnum
Fast growing, shrubby deciduous trees, flowering in spring.
Large branches heal only slowly but laburnums can take a fair amount of pruning, immediately after bloom being the best time. For a tree, give it the usual early training, and occasionally cut out dead or wayward branches that are crowding the tree's centre and distracting from its shape. For a large shrub, cut back the leader of the young plant to f   le stems. Laburnums m   nteresting espaliers and can be trained over arches. Prune these by removing wayward branches at the usual pruning time. You may want to cut off the seed pods, which are poisonous and make a mess when they drop.
Propagation Easy, from seed in autumn. Selected hybrids such as 'Vossi' are best budded onto seedling understocks in

summer, as they don't come true from seed.

GOLDEN RAIN TREE,
willow pattern tree
Koelreuteria
Deciduous trees, flowering in summer months.
Young trees need careful training to develop a single trunk and to avoid weak, V-shaped crotches, but established trees need no pruning other than removal of dead wood. You may want to remove the lowest branches as the tree develops, but be careful not to spoil its graceful shape. The inflated seed pods can be cut off after they turn brown.
Propagation Easy, by seed sown in autumn (it probably won't germinate until spring) or root cuttings in winter.

GORDONIA
Gordonia axillaris
Slow growing, evergreen tree, flowering from autumn to spring.
Like its close relatives the camellias, the gordonia starts as an upright shrub, maturing to a handsome, short-boled tree with long, ascending branches and a spreading crown. Remove the lower branches (in winter) as it matures. It can be kept as a shrub by occasional heading back, quite hard if need be, in late winter or early spring before growth begins.
Propagation Quite easy, by half-ripe cuttings or by layering in summer.

HACKBERRY, sugarberry
Celtis
Deciduous trees.
Young trees benefit from the usual training to ensure a reasonably long stem, but established trees, although they can take heavy pruning, rarely need more than removal of

dead wood. If a tree is too dense and shady, it can be opened up by selectively cutting excess branches back to main limbs or to the trunk; you can do this either in winter or in late summer when growth has stopped.

Propagation Easy, from seed sown in autumn or spring.

HAWTHORN, English may
Crataegus
Deciduous trees, often shrubby, flowering in spring and bearing berries (haws) in autumn/winter.

Most species are naturally multi-trunked trees, but they are easy to train to single stems if you want. They tend to have very bushy crowns; limit the young tree to four or five branches to forestall overcrowding later. The English hawthorns (*C. oxyacantha* and *C. monogyna*) are traditional plants for rural hedges. English hedgerows are 'laid' (see Hedges on page 12). It is easier to plant your trees about a metre apart and clip them as for any other hedge. They will flower and fruit reasonably well. Wear stout gloves against the thorns.

Propagation Fairly easy, from seed sown in autumn (it won't germinate until spring). Cultivars such as 'Paul's Scarlet' are budded in late summer on seedling stock.

HAZEL, filbert
Corylus
Shrubby, deciduous trees, flowering in spring.

All the hazels grow naturally with several trunks, and it is a lot of bother to train them to a single stem as they sucker constantly. Whether you are growing them for ornament or for the nuts, the only pruning needed is thinning out a few of the oldest stems every other winter or so. The wriggle-branched crazy filbert (*C. avellana* 'Contorta') is often grafted onto seedlings of the regular type, and you need to watch for suckers from the understock. Pull these off as soon as you notice them. Filberts are prone to stem cankers; if they appear, cut the branch back into healthy wood at once, and sterilise your pruning tools between cuts.

Propagation Easy, if a little complicated. In spring, mound about 25 cm of soft earth over the base of the tree and keep it

'Laying' a hawthorn hedge involved breaking the branches half through and weaving them together like so much basket work. Clipped normally, this hawthorn hedge at Whitley, Sutton Forest, NSW, is less impenetrable, but effective just the same.

moist. This will encourage suckers to appear and root; by winter they should be rooted and ready to transplant. Layering in spring is a simpler alternative for a few plants.

HONEY LOCUST
Gleditsia triacanthos
Fast growing, deciduous tree; the spring flowers are unimportant.
Young trees need careful training to establish a clean stem and strong, well-placed main branches. Don't cut the side branches off a newly planted tree; head them back to about 20 cm and cut them flush the following year. Remove any thorny suckers. Once the framework is established, all you need to do is thin out overcrowded and crossing branches, and any that are forming weak, V-shaped crotches. Winter is the main pruning time. 'Sunburst' tends to make long, semi-weeping branches; if they hang too low, you can trim them up in summer. Grow a named, thornless variety; even the trunk of the wild tree is viciously spiky. Remove seed pods from young trees to prevent wasting energy.
Propagation Easy, from autumn-sown seed, although most of the seedlings will be thorny. Discard these, or use them as understock on which you can bud a named variety in late summer.

HOOP PINE
Araucaria cunninghamii
Large coniferous evergreen tree. Naturally shapely, this does not need regular pruning. Young trees sometimes develop double leaders; cut out the weaker of the two in winter. Make any cuts right back to another branch to prevent die back of the stump.
Propagation Fairly easy, by seed in summer.

HORSE CHESTNUT
Aesculus
Slow growing, deciduous trees, flowering in summer.
Young trees should be trained to a single leader, but established trees need no pruning other than the removal of dead or damaged branches. Winter is the best time for this clearing out of the tree.
Propagation Fairly easy, from seed in spring or by grafting selected varieties onto seedling stock in winter.

Left unpruned except for the removal of a few low branches, this old hazel at Nine Mile Garden, Stanley, Vic., has grown large enough to shelter a table and chairs.

The hoop pine is big for the average garden but develops symmetrically.

The Illawarra flame tree bears flowers on branches that drop leaves in spring.

The Indian laburnum is the sub-tropics' answer to Europe's golden chain tree.

The Irish strawberry tree is indeed native to Ireland.

The jacaranda varies in size with climate. These are in Sydney and are not too big for a suburban backyard; in the sub-tropics they can be twice the size and need a big space. You can't prune jacarandas small without losing the flowers.

ILLAWARRA FLAME TREE
Brachychiton acerifolius
Deciduous tree, flowering in summer months.

These trees will take hard pruning but in gardens they should be left alone except for the occasional removal of dead and/or damaged branches. Naturally shapely, young trees rarely need training.

Propagation Quite easy from seed sown in spring or autumn but seedlings are often unreliable, putting on a show only once every few years; it is better to graft scions from a known free-flowering tree on seedling stocks, or at least to save the seed from a tree you know is reliable.

INCENSE CEDAR
Calocedrus decurrens
Evergreen, coniferous tree, random branching.

Naturally symmetrical and pyramidal in habit, the incense cedar needs no pruning. As the tree matures, the lowest branches can be removed to reveal the handsome trunk. In its native California, it is grown for tall hedges, which are sheared as needed during the summer months.

Propagation Easy, from cuttings in late summer. Seed sown in autumn germinates well but is not often available.

INDIAN BEAN TREE
Catalpa bignonioides
Fast growing, deciduous tree, flowering in summer.

You need to train young trees carefully to a tall central leader; their natural habit is to branch very low. Stake the leader, and pinch out side shoots as they develop, until the trunk is as long as you wish, cutting them right off when the crown has begun to develop, after two or three

years. Established trees need only the occasional removal of dead or badly placed branches. Best pruning time is in winter.

Propagation Fairly easy, from seed in spring or cuttings of side shoots in late summer, the best way to propagate the golden-leafed form 'Aurea'.

INDIAN LABURNUM
Cassia fistula
Deciduous tree, flowering in spring months.

The Indian laburnum can be headed back after bloom to keep it compact, but normally all it needs is the occasional removal of dead wood.

Propagation Easy, from fresh seed soaked and sown in spring.

IRISH STRAWBERRY TREE
Arbutus unedo
Slow growing, evergreen trees or large shrubs, flowering in summer months.

The strawberry tree is naturally multi-stemmed but can be trained to a single trunk. As the tree develops, removal of the lowest and twiggiest small branches will reveal the lines and attractive bark of the main limbs. Heading back will keep the plant as a tall shrub.

Propagation Fairly easy, by semi-hardwood cuttings in early autumn, or from seed sown in autumn or spring.

JACARANDA
Jacaranda mimosifolia
Fast growing, deciduous tree, flowering in summer.

Jacarandas will take heavy lopping in winter but it will ruin the graceful shape of the tree and prevent flowering for at least three years. Therefore, don't prune, but you can remove dead wood when you notice it. Young trees may need shaping, but go easy— they almost always settle down

to shapely maturity without any assistance.

Propagation Very easy, from seed sown in spring.

JAPANESE CEDAR
Cryptomeria japonica
Evergreen coniferous tree, whorl branching type.

The most commonly grown variety is 'Elegans'. It makes a broad pyramid of fluffy, juvenile foliage, so dense and borne on so many secondary branches that the rather flexible wood is apt to bend under its weight so that the tree almost always leans. Judicious thinning of the branches, to open up the tree and create a tiered effect, can keep it straight but alters its character. You may prefer to remove only dead wood and let the tree lean if it wishes.

Propagation Fairly easy, by cuttings in late summer.

JAPANESE ELM
Zelkova
Fairly fast growing, deciduous tree. Flowers unimportant; graceful habit and fine foliage are the features.

This graceful multi-stemmed tree needs only the removal of too low branches in winter, and maybe an occasional thinning of the crown should it become too dense. It looks splendid on a single trunk, but needs careful training.

Propagation Fairly easy, from autumn-sown seed in cool areas. In warmer areas, store seed in refrigerator (not freezer) and sow in spring.

JUDAS TREE, redbud
Cercis
Slow growing, deciduous trees, flowering in spring.

Naturally multi-stemmed, this can be trained as a single-stemmed tree, but after initial training needs no regular pruning other than removal of dead wood. Lower branches can be removed from established trees to reveal the trunks. This is best done in winter, but you can delay until the buds are about to open and use them as cut flowers.

Propagation Easy if slow, from seed sown in autumn; selected varieties such as the white Judas tree are budded on seedling stock in late summer. If branches are low enough, they can be layered in spring.

KAURI
Agathis
Fairly slow growing, coniferous, evergreen trees, whorl branching.
Young trees can develop a double leader; remove the weaker. Established trees need only removal of dead branches.
Propagation Easy, by seed sown in spring.

KOWHAI
Sophora tetraptera
Evergreen or deciduous tree or large shrub, flowering in spring.
The kowhai, New Zealand's national flower, can be a large shrub or a small, multi-stemmed tree, and it can also be trained as a single-stemmed tree if you prefer. (It tends to be tree-sized in warm areas, shrub-sized in cool.) Once past its initial training, it needs only the occasional wayward branch headed back to keep it shapely. After bloom is the best time.
Propagation Easy, by seed sown in spring.

KURRAJONG
Brachychiton populneus
Deciduous tree, flowering in spring and summer.
Kurrajongs will take hard pruning and are sometimes lopped to provide emergency

fodder for cattle. In gardens, they should be left alone except for the removal of any dead or damaged branches. Naturally shapely, young trees rarely need training.
Propagation Quite easy, from seed sown in spring or autumn.

LEYLAND CYPRESS
Cupressocyparis leylandii
Coniferous, evergreen tree, random branching.
The leyland cypress is often grown as a fast, tall hedge, for which it is well suited as it takes frequent shearing very readily. But don't try to make your hedge too narrow and don't cut into bare wood, which won't sprout. Free growing trees (which become very large) need no pruning other than occasional clearing out of dead wood.
Propagation Fairly easy, by cuttings in late summer.

LILLYPILLY
Acmena
Fairly fast growing, evergreen trees, flowering in spring.
Young trees may need awkwardly placed limbs shortened to bring the tree into balance; mature trees only need removal of dead or damaged wood. They are dense growers; if their shade is too heavy, the crown can be lightly thinned out in late summer. Young trees can be clipped as tall hedges or topiary, but this will reduce the amount of flowers and fruit. (You do get handsomely tinted young growth.)
Propagation Easy, by seed in spring or summer.

LIQUIDAMBAR
Liquidambar
Fast growing, deciduous trees, grown for their autumn foliage.
Broadly pyramidal when young, liquidambars develop a

more rounded crown with maturity. Young trees sometimes develop double leaders, which should be corrected by cutting out the weaker. They branch low and look very handsome with their skirts sweeping the ground; but if you want to walk under the tree, pinch back the lower branches to divert their energy to the leader. Don't start removing them until the tree is at least four years old, and then raise the crown gradually—removing the branches too early can lead to a weak, crooked trunk. Otherwise no regular pruning is needed. They will grow back strongly if cut hard, but don't try to control size or shape that way—all you'll do is spoil the tree's fine shape. Don't cut the roots, or they will sucker.
Propagation Easy, from seed in autumn. Select your seed only from trees of fine colour, and discard seedlings that don't show good autumn colour from the start. They'll never improve. Selected colour forms such as 'Festeri' are budded in spring on selected seedling stocks.

LOQUAT
Eriobotrya japonica
Evergreen tree, grown for its winter/spring fruit.
Loquat trees tend to grow with several trunks, but with early training they can be held to a single one. The crown tends to be very dense, and some thinning to remove the weaker branches will let in more light. It also increases the size of the individual fruit and lightens the load on the limbs, which are a bit brittle. The tree can take hard pruning and makes a striking espalier. Prune in early spring after harvest but before growth begins again.

Propagation Easy, from seed sown in spring, but seedlings are unreliable and it is better to graft from a named variety onto seedling stock. You might also try half-ripe cuttings in late summer.

LYCHEE
Litchi chinensis
Slow growing, evergreen tree, flowering in spring but grown for its summer fruit.

The lychee is naturally multi-stemmed, but you can train trees to single trunks if you wish. By tradition, you prune by cutting the bunches of fruit with long stems like flowers, but you may also want to thin out weak and overcrowded growth occasionally, making all your cuts to a lateral or the main stem.

Propagation Fairly easy. Air-layering in summer is the traditional method, but half-ripe cuttings taken in late summer can be tried. Seed germinates very easily if sown as soon as the fruit is ripe, but these seedling trees are unreliable in the extreme.

MACADAMIA,
Queensland nut
Macadamia
Evergreen tree, flowering in spring months.

Young trees tend to bushiness and benefit from staking to ensure the main branches are well spaced. Established trees need no regular pruning, but if you have to remove a broken or wayward branch, cut back to a lateral—bare wood does not usually sprout. Macadamia trees are best pruned at the end of autumn.

Propagation Fairly easy. Seed sown in autumn or spring germinates easily, but for the most reliable crop it is really best to bud or graft a named

It isn't really possible to keep a cypress hedge smaller than this one at Whitley, Sutton Forest, NSW; the tree would grow to 30 m tall if given its head.

The prettily coloured young foliage of the lillypilly made it a favourite hedging plant in colonial times, and the idea is worth reviving.

variety onto the seedling stock in late spring.

MAGNOLIA
Magnolia

Fairly slow growing, deciduous or evergreen trees and shrubs, flowering in spring or summer.

Magnolias don't really like being pruned, and the rule is to do as little as possible, except for removing dead or damaged wood. If you do prune, cut branches back to strong laterals or to the base, leaving no stubs to rot. The deciduous, spring flowering types are mostly rather shrubby trees (*M. stellata* is a spreading shrub). You can remove lower branches to raise the crown and thin branches a bit if they get too dense (best times are just as they are coming into bloom or in summer after growth has finished). They will look awkward if trained on single trunks. Don't leave the job too late—it is best to remove branches before they get too large, and to pinch back shoots that look as though they will grow where they shouldn't. *M. liliflora* is naturally low branching and spreading, and it is difficult to make it grow tall and tree-like. *M. soulangeana* and *M. denudata (heptapeta)* are more amenable. The evergreen *M. grandiflora* will grow into a majestic, spreading tree with the removal of dead branches, but you can gently shape a young tree by heading back wayward branches if needed, best time being in late summer.

Propagation Slow and not very easy; the best way in the garden is by layering in spring. Seed sown in autumn as soon as it is ripe germinates easily, but the seedlings may take their time about flowering.

MAIDENHAIR TREE
Gingko biloba

Slow growing, deciduous tree.

Ginkgos often go through an awkward adolescence, sending out one or two very long branches that unbalance their shape. With time, they will fill out, but you can help the process by shortening the rogue branch to a well-placed lateral or cutting it back to the trunk if it is too low down. Otherwise, they need no pruning other than removal of dead or very weak branches. Winter is the best pruning time.

Propagation By hardwood cuttings in winter. Autumn-sown seed grows quickly, but cuttings give trees of known sex. (The fruit is often not wanted because of its strong, cheesy odour, but the roasted seeds are a great delicacy.)

MANGO
Mangifera indica

Evergreen tree, flowering in spring and grown for its fruit.

A young mango needs only the usual training to ensure it grows into a shapely tree. Established trees need no routine pruning, but you may want to thin out some branches from the interior of the tree if they become crowded. Best time to prune is after harvest. If the tree falls into the habit of only bearing every other year, drastic thinning of the half-ripe crop in an 'on' year may cure it.

Propagation Fairly easy. Seed sown as soon as the fruit is ripe germinates easily and

Grafted, named varieties of mango are usually smaller than seedling trees.

A young plant of Magnolia stellata *about the age when it begins to spread.*

This maidenhair tree is about ten years old and beginning to fill out.

Normally rather shrubby, Magnolia soulangeana *can be trained as a multi-stemmed tree as here by selectively removing lower branches. The vertical shoots from the base (centre of picture) would be better removed.*

The long branches of a young mulberry need to be shortened to produce a compact tree. Cut back to a lateral or an upward-facing bud.

The New South Wales Christmas bush is naturally a small upright tree.

The lowest branches of this native frangipani could be removed.

This is the ordinary, seed-propagated Japanese maple, Acer palmatum, a slow grower to about 5 m. It needs little pruning other than removing dead branches.

quickly. Each seed will produce several shoots; when they appear, gently separate the individual plants. Then graft a good, named variety on each.

MAPLE
Acer
Deciduous trees and shrubs.
Little pruning is needed other than the removal of dead or crowded branches and maybe the thinning of the crown to reveal the tree's graceful habit. Don't try to control size by heading back; they don't take kindly to it and the shape of the tree will be spoilt. *A. palmatum* usually grows as a rather shrubby, multi-trunked tree; selective removal of the lowest branches will raise the crown sufficiently to allow walking beneath it. Remove dead wood at any time, but other pruning is best done immediately the leaves have fallen or in late summer when growth has stopped; if you prune either just before or during growth, the plants will bleed uncontrollably.
Propagation Fairly easy, by seed sown in spring. Fancy-leaved varieties are budded or grafted in late spring onto seedling stock.

MULBERRY
Morus
Fast growing, deciduous trees, flowering in spring.
Mulberries make long, limber branches that give them a semi-weeping habit, and young trees need careful staking and training to achieve a reasonably long trunk and well-shaped crown. Stake the leader to the height you want, and in the first couple of years shorten long, waving branches either back to a lateral or to an upward-facing bud to encourage the tree to grow bushier.

How you treat an established tree depends on whether you are primarily interested in shade or the fruit. Shade trees can be thinned and have any over-long branches shortened back in winter; fruiting mulberries can be thinned in winter, but heading back is best left until after harvest. The black mulberry, *M. nigra*, is not only choicer than the white (*M. alba*), it grows more slowly and needs less pruning. (The white, on the other hand, is the one for silkworms.)

Propagation The white mulberry is easy from hardwood cuttings taken in late autumn or winter. The black is trickier and is normally grafted on root cuttings of the white mulberry, but you might try layering in autumn or budding in late spring on cutting-grown white mulberry seedlings.

NATIVE FRANGIPANI,
sweetshade, woolum
Hymenosporum flavum
Evergreen tree, flowering during late spring.
No regular pruning is needed, apart from removal of dead wood. Branching is normally sparse and open; to make young trees bushier, pinch young growth or plant two or three together to make a multi-stemmed clump.

Propagation Easy, by spring- or autumn-sown seed or softwood cuttings in summer.

NEW SOUTH WALES CHRISTMAS BUSH
Ceratopetalum gummiferum
Evergreen tree or large shrub, flowering in late spring.
This benefits from heading back after bloom to encourage plenty of fresh growth, which will flower next year.

Propagation Easy, from fresh seed sown in autumn. Choose seed from free-blooming, well-coloured plants for the best results with this plant.

NORFOLK ISLAND HIBISCUS,
cow itch tree, pyramid tree
Lagunaria patersonii
Slow growing, evergreen tree, flowering in summer.
Although it can take fairly heavy pruning (and be used as a tall clipped hedge), this valuable seaside tree rarely needs anything other than the removal of dead wood. If it gets too shady, thin the crown in late summer after flowering, but wear gloves—sharp hairs on the seed pods can cause skin irritation.

Propagation Easy, by seed sown in spring or half-ripe cuttings in summer.

NORFOLK ISLAND PINE
Araucaria heterophylla
Large coniferous evergreen tree.
No regular pruning needed. Young trees can develop double leaders; cut out the weaker of the two in winter.

Propagation Fairly easy, by seed in summer.

OAK
Quercus
Slow growing, deciduous or evergreen trees.
Young oaks tend to grow as bushes full of twigs. To encourage them to grow tall sooner, pinch back side shoots to channel the plant's energy into the leader; but don't remove the side branches until the tree has gained some height and the framework of branches has begun to develop. If a double leader develops, cut the weaker one out. The young pin oak (*Q. palustris*) has flexible branches, and if you remove the lowest so that you can walk under it, the next tier will bend down to fill its place.

Raising the crown is best left until the tree begins to lose the pyramidal outline of adolescence. (*Q. lobata* has the same habit.) Once past the early training, oaks need little attention, but you may want to thin out crowded branches from time to time in winter or late summer. Always cut back to a fork—if you cut part way, the result is quite likely to be a brush of twigs.

The evergreen *Q. ilex* will take clipping and is sometimes used for tall formal hedges, but it is naturally a substantial tree. Give it the same early training as the deciduous species and thin the crown of mature trees from time to time if they get over-bushy and gloomy. The best time to thin is late summer.

Propagation Easy, from seed sown as soon as it is ripe (it loses viability quickly) during autumn months.

OLIVE
Olea europaea
Slow growing, evergreen tree, flowering in spring.
The olive is one of the longest lived trees, and unless you train young plants with care they will remain as shrubs for years. The tree can be trained with a single trunk or three or four: stake your selected main shoot(s), pinch back the side shoots and ruthlessly pull off any suckers from the base as soon as they appear. Once the desired structure of main trunks and branches is achieved, the trees need no pruning, but if growth is so luxuriant that you can't see the lines of the branches, you can thin out unwanted growth after harvest. The wild olive (*O. africana*) is not grown for its fruit but as a shade tree or tall hedge. To grow it as a tree,

train as for the fruiting olive but thin in early spring, to reduce the number of seeds and unwanted seedlings. Hedges are given the usual treatment.

Propagation Easy, from seed sown in autumn, but if you want good quality fruit it is much better to take cuttings in early winter.

ORCHID TREE
Bauhinia variegata
Evergreen or partly deciduous tree flowering in spring.

The orchid tree, with pink or white flowers, is naturally shrubby and multi-stemmed in habit, but young trees can be trained easily to single trunks. Once established, it needs no pruning other than occasional removal of weak wood. It is sometimes pollarded after bloom, but that ruins its natural elegance of habit.

Propagation Usually from seed sown in summer, but summer cuttings root quite easily.

PAGODA TREE
Sophora japonica
Deciduous tree, flowering in summer months.

The pagoda tree needs only routine training in its youth;

you can grow it either single- or multi-stemmed. As it is a fairly big shady tree, single-stemmed is usually best. Mature, it needs no regular pruning apart from removal of dead branches from inside the crown. Do any pruning necessary in late winter.

Propagation Easy, by seed sown in spring.

PALMS
Evergreen trees, usually single-stemmed but sometimes forming into clumps.

Palms need only the removal of dead leaves and flower clusters, for neatness. Don't try to strip a dead leaf right off; cut it close to the trunk and let the leaf base fall off when the plant is ready to shed it. Go carefully; many palms have thorns on the lower parts of the leaf stalks.

Propagation Quite easy, from spring-sown seed, but may take up to two years to germinate. Most germinate and grow faster in a greenhouse. Some clump-forming types such as rhapis and chamaedoreas can be increased by carefully removing any rooted suckers in spring.

PEACH, nectarine
Prunus persica cultivars
Fairly fast growing, deciduous trees, flowering in spring.

Peaches and nectarines are the fastest growing of the deciduous fruit trees. Prune to keep the trees compact; unpruned, they will still fruit well, but as each shoot only bears once, the fruit will be borne further and further out from the main trunk and branches may break under the weight of the crop. Young trees should have their side shoots trimmed fairly hard at planting, and for the first couple of years you pinch back excess side shoots as they grow. Once fruiting has commenced, it is traditional to prune fairly hard in winter, but you can do the job in summer immediately after harvest. Remove about two-thirds of the wood that has fruited, thinning out some shoots altogether and heading back others about halfway to two-thirds. This should leave enough new shoots in place to bear next year's crop.

Young flowering peaches need the usual training to ensure a strong stem and well-spaced branches, but then they

The lacquer palm, a clump former, is strictly for tropical climates.

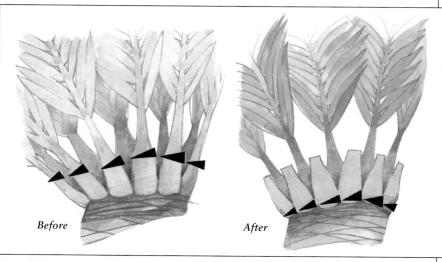

Before *After*

Cut off the lowest fronds of a palm close to their bases. The bases will die and fall off, or they can be cut off flush with the trunk next year.

need little pruning other than occasional thinning out of overcrowded growth. The best time for this is early in the flowering period, so that you can use the prunings in vases, or immediately after bloom; but you can also prune in winter. They are traditionally pruned hard (pollarded) immediately after bloom but can be allowed to grow naturally, simply thinning out weak shoots or those that interfere with the tree's shape. Both flowering and fruiting peaches can be trained as espaliers, the fan-shape being the easiest to form and maintain.

Propagation Named varieties are usually budded in summer on seedling stocks, grown from seed sown the previous autumn, but they can be grown from hardwood cuttings in late autumn. Seedlings are apt to be of inferior quality.

PEAR
Pyrus communis and
P. pyrifolia cultivars
Fairly fast growing, deciduous trees, flowering in spring.
Pears are closely related to apples, and like them bear their flowers and fruit on short spurs that flower for several years. Their pruning is much the same, but the trees are stronger and larger in growth. In the first three or four years, pruning is done in winter and aims to create a well-balanced framework of branches. Once fruiting has begun, most pruning is done in summer. Pears are inclined to make strong, upright shoots in the centre of the tree; cut out all that you don't want to make new fruiting branches, when you notice them. An overgrown tree can be renewed by cutting it back hard to the main framework in winter, and then shortening the

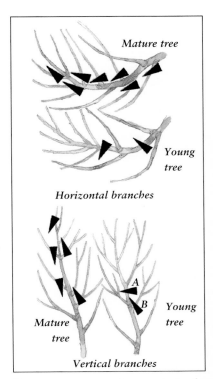

Prune a mature peach or nectarine by removing about two-thirds of last year's growth. Young trees need more care: on a vertical branch a cut at A widens the tree; one at B extends it up.

This Canary Island date palm would be handsomer for an annual clean up of the dead leaves.

Regular summer pruning of pears encourages the fruit to grow on compact spurs like those at the top of the picture, rather than on the long weak shoots at the bottom.

Pepper tree fruit can be dried and used as a spice but is inferior to real pepper.

A pear tree produces many upright stems to crowd out the centre. Remove all but a few that will produce new fruiting spurs.

A fine old tree like this pepper tree needs no pruning, except a trim of any twigs that hang too low. Place the tree with care, as it has strong surface roots.

Pyramidal in youth, Pinus radiata pine trees, such as these at Durham Hall, Braidwood, NSW, develop spreading shapes as they mature.

strong shoots that result in summer; but it will be a couple of years before you have a crop. Like apples, pears can be trained in all the various styles of espalier, and they can be trained over an arch or pergola, when your main job will be cutting back the upright shoots as they arise in summer.

The nashi or Japanese pear (*Pyrus pyrifolia*) is pruned in the same way as the European pears. It is a slightly smaller tree, and does well in warmer climates than the European pears prefer. It has the advantage, too, of being self-fertile, so that you don't need two trees for fruit.

The various flowering pears (*P. calleryana*, *P. ussuriensis*, *P. salicifolia* and others) need only initial training to ensure a shapely tree and the occasional removal after bloom of weak or overcrowded branches. Cut back to main stems or laterals; stumps will produce bunches of new shoots and the last state will be more crowded than the first. The willow-leaved or silver pear (*P. salicifolia*) is usually grown in its weeping form, which needs firm staking until the leader has grown as tall as you want it.

Propagation Not really easy. The best method is budding in summer, either on pear seedlings, selected pear stocks (grown from root cuttings) or seedling quinces, which give a smaller tree. The flowering pears can be grown fairly easily from seed or hardwood cuttings in autumn, but cutting-grown fruiting pears are apt to be too vigorous and delayed in coming into bearing for most gardens.

The ornamental pears are often grown from seed, but cutting-grown plants are better as they will all be the same clone.

PECAN
Carya illinoinensis
Deciduous tree, flowering in spring months.
Young trees need only the usual training; established trees need no pruning other than the occasional removal of dead, damaged or over-crowded limbs, which may be done at any time except during the full spring flush of growth.
Propagation Fresh seed germinates easily, but it is better to bud a named variety onto seedling stock—seedlings are unreliable bearers and need cross-pollination for bearing. Few pecans are self-fertile.

PEPPER TREE
Schinus ariera
Fast growing, evergreen tree, flowering in late spring.
The pepper tree is loved for its picturesque, gnarled branches and its gracefully weeping foliage, but to achieve a tree with a crown high enough to walk under, it must have careful training in its youth; cut into branches that have grown thicker than 8 cm or so and you are inviting rot. Stake the leader securely, and pinch back unwanted side shoots until the trunk is as tall as you want it. Established trees are best pruned as little as possible; but if you must cut out a wayward branch or two, do it in early spring and cut to a strong lateral. As long as you don't cut into developed wood, you can use the pepper tree as a big, informal hedge. Set the young plants about a metre apart, pinch them to make them bushy and multi-stemmed, then trim foliage as needed to keep the hedge the size you want.
Propagation Easy, and most commonly, by spring-sown seed. Half-ripe cuttings taken in summer should root readily.

PERSIMMON
Diospyros kaki
Fairly fast growing, deciduous tree, flowering in summer and grown for fruit and for its autumn foliage.
Young persimmon trees are inclined to make weak crotches and need training to form a good framework of well-spaced branches, growing out at wide angles from the trunk, which will probably need staking for the first couple of years. After that, prune as little as possible, in order not to spoil the tree's graceful shape. Dead wood will need to be removed, and every so often (in winter) you might want to cut the odd wayward branch or watersprout back to a strong lateral.
Propagation Quite easily, from autumn-sown seed, but seedlings are very unreliable (they are apt to come in male and female) and it is better to bud a named, hermaphrodite variety in summer on seedling rootstock. If your tree branches to the ground, you can try layering it in summer.

PINE
Pinus
Fast growing, evergreen coniferous trees, whorl branching.
Pines rarely need pruning, but you may need to cut out a double leader that threatens to spoil the shape and remove dead lower branches as the tree matures. You can control growth to some extent by pruning the 'candles' of new growth as they develop, the right time being when the shoot has grown to full length but before the needles have unfurled. If you remove the candle entirely, you hold the branch at that length (new shoots will grow from its base next year); trim it part way,

and it will form a new terminal bud that will grow a single new shoot next year.
You can thin an over-dense pine (the best time being in early spring), cutting your unwanted branches to strong laterals or the main trunk. The Japanese have developed the art of pruning pines to reveal the lines of the main branches to a fine art; but remember that new growth from bare wood is unlikely and go carefully; if you remove a branch and leave a gaping hole in your tree you may have to look at it for many years.
Propagation Easy, from spring-sown seed.

PINK SHOWER
Cassia grandis
Deciduous tree, flowering in summer months.
These trees can be headed back after bloom to keep them compact, but normally all they need is the occasional removal of dead wood.
Propagation Easy, from fresh seed sown in spring. Soak it before planting.

PISTACHIO, pistache
Pistacia
Deciduous trees, flowering in spring months.
Whether you are growing the true pistachio (*P. vera*) for its nuts or the Chinese pistache (*P. chinensis*) for its autumn foliage, prune as little as possible. Young trees are apt to grow over-bushy and may need crowded branches removed, and you may need to thin mature trees occasionally also (the best time is late winter), but annual attention is not usually needed.
Propagation The ornamental species are easily grown from seed sown in autumn, but seedlings grow slowly in the

beginning. Select the best coloured ones for growing on. Fruiting pistachios are best budded in late spring on seedling stock; seedling trees are inclined to bear all male or all female flowers, and you won't know which is which until they flower, which takes several years.

PITTOSPORUM
Pittosporum
Fast growing, evergreen trees and shrubs, flowering in summer.
The pittosporums fall into two main groups: small trees such as *P. rhombifolium*, *P. undulatum* and *P. phillyraeoides*, and shrubs of various sizes, of which the best known are *P. eugenioides*, *P. tobira* and *P. tenuifolium*. The tree types are shrubby in growth and will probably need some removal of the lower branches as they mature to reveal their trunks. *P. undulatum* is inclined to grow very dense and looks best if you thin the crown to let in some light every couple of years, the best time being in winter. The shrubs need little pruning other than removal of the occasional dead or wayward branch, but they can be sheared to make hedges and simple topiary. (The trees also, but it would be a shame to spoil the graceful, weeping habit of *P. phillyraeoides* by shearing it.) The leaves of *P. tenuifolium* are used for flower arranging; you may want to cut the plants back fairly hard every couple of winters to encourage long sprays of new growth.
Propagation Easy, from seed in spring or half-ripe cuttings (the best way for the fancy-leaved varieties) in summer. *P. undulatum* comes up very readily from self-sown seed, and can be a pest.

PLANE
Platanus
Fast growing, deciduous trees, flowering in spring but mainly grown for shade.
Young trees may need training to ensure a tall, straight leader—pinch back side shoots in summer and trim them off in winter. Rub off unwanted shoots from the trunks of young trees as they appear. Once the trees are established they need no regular pruning. They do, however, respond very strongly to it, and pollarded planes are familiar as street trees in Europe (in Australia, butchered planes are commoner!). You can thin the crowns if they are too dense and shady, a job for a tree surgeon as these are big trees. In some areas, planes are prone to anthracnose, a disease that causes die back of young shoots. Affected shoots should be cut off and burnt.
Propagation Easy, by seed in autumn or hardwood cuttings in winter. Seedlings are somewhat variable; cuttings must be used if you are propagating a selected form such as the Cyprus plane.

PLUM
Prunus domestica
Fairly fast growing, deciduous trees, flowering in spring.
Fruiting plums fall into two groups, the European and Japanese. Japanese plums include 'Satsuma', 'Santa Rosa' and 'Narrabeen'; Europeans include 'Angelina Burdett', 'Greengage' and 'Grand Duke'. Both types bear most of their fruit on short spurs and need the usual early training to establish a strong framework. Then, Japanese plums need winter pruning to control size and shape. Thin out and head back last summer's over-long shoots, cutting to a lateral or right out. Whether you leave mostly vertical or horizontal shoots depends on whether the tree is naturally upright or a sprawler. Once the European plums have settled into bearing, they are treated similarly; but as they make much less new growth they need less attention. An unpruned plum tree in bloom is a lovely sight and the temptation to leave it be is great. But in later years you may need to prop up the spreading branches lest they break under the weight of fruit. Many varieties make short, thorn-like stems. Don't cut them out, as they will develop into fruiting spurs; just snip off the sharp tip. Most varieties benefit from crop thinning when the developing fruit are about the size of marbles.

The ornamental plums, including the purple-leaved plums (*P. cerasifera* forms), are all treated much more simply. Young trees need the usual training to ensure a strong stem and well-spaced branches, but then they need little pruning other than occasional thinning out of overcrowded growth. The best time is early in the flowering period or immediately after bloom; but there will be no harm done if you prefer to do it in winter.
Propagation Fairly easily, from hardwood cuttings in winter, usually budded onto myrabolan plum understocks. Ornamental plums can be grown from seed sown in autumn—the purple-leaved plums usually come up true and the cherry plum, their green-leaved version, often comes up unbidden. (Its fruit is less richly flavoured than the European and Japanese plums, but it makes good jam and is useful as an understock.)

The London plane (Platanus hispanica) *heals its wounds easily, without too much scarring of its beautiful bark. But that is no excuse for careless pruning! No matter how hard you prune, do the job properly.*

The Lombardy poplar usually branches (and suckers) right from the base—these have been trimmed in their youth by sheep. Some regular cleaning up of their feet is desirable to control their habit of suckering.

PODOCARPS
Podocarpus
Slow growing, evergreen conifers, random branching.

The podocarps vary from small shrubs to fairly substantial trees, which can be trained to either one or several trunks; all are elegant growers that need little pruning, other than occasional shortening of an overlong branch. They are unusual among conifers as they grow back when cut into bare wood and can take quite a lot of pruning if you want to control their size or shape. They can be clipped as hedges or topiary, or 'cloud pruned' in the Japanese manner. Best time for pruning is in spring, before growth begins, or in summer, after it is over; shear hedges at any time.

Propagation Easy, from seed in spring or autumn, or layering or half-ripe cuttings taken in summer.

POINCIANA, flamboyant tree
Delonix regia
Fast growing, semi-deciduous tree, flowering in late spring.

Trees may need early training to establish a single tall stem, but established trees need only removal of dead or broken branches, cutting always to another branch; stubs rarely grow. Outside branches tend to weep, and if they grow too low can be shortened. Prune at any time, but after flowering is most effective.

Propagation Easy, from fresh seed sown during summer or in autumn months.

POPLAR
Populus
Fast growing, deciduous trees.
Poplars are big, greedy-rooted trees, notorious for clogging sewers and damaging buildings and paving. They need only

removal of dead wood and the suckers that they almost all produce in great numbers, especially if the roots are cut. They will grow back strongly after hard winter pruning but this usually spoils the shape. Most species become dangerously brittle with age and need professional attention to keep them stable.

Propagation Very easy, by hardwood cuttings in winter. Quite large branches will take root in ground that is kept constantly moist.

PRINCESS TREE, powton
Paulownia
Fast growing, deciduous trees, flowering in spring.

These trees grow very fast for the first few years. Stake them for the first summer or two and pinch out any side shoots to encourage the leader to grow tall; when the stem is as tall as you want, allow the branches to develop. Then just thin out dead wood and any that is too weak to flower. Do this in winter, when the flower buds will already be well developed. The trees will take heavy lopping and can be pollarded or even cut virtually to the ground each year. This keeps them at shrub size. They will then produce enormous leaves, but no flowers; and in our mild climate there are better plants if you want the huge-leaved tropical look.

Propagation Easy, from root cuttings taken in winter, the usual method, or from seed sown in spring.

QUEENSLAND LACEBARK
Brachychiton discolor
Summer deciduous trees, flowering in summer.
Treat as for the kurrajong tree.
Propagation Quite easy, from seed sown in spring or autumn.

QUINCE
Cydonia oblonga
Deciduous tree, flowering in spring months.

The quince tends to be shrubby in growth; young trees need careful training to form a single trunk and well-spaced framework of branches, but a multi-stemmed tree is handsome and will bear well. An established tree needs only clearing out of the spindly shoots in the centre of the tree every couple of winters; the more light and air you can admit to the young growth the heavier your crop will be. Grown quinces tend to sucker madly; remove the suckers as you see them developing.

Propagation Hardwood cuttings taken in winter strike easily but are apt to sucker; sowing seed in autumn and then budding a named variety onto the seedlings in their second spring gives a more manageable tree.

RAIN TREE
Samanea saman
Fast growing, more-or-less evergreen tree, flowering in summer.
This tree is only for the tropics, where it is the finest of all street and shade trees. Young trees may need staking and training to a single stem but established trees rarely need pruning. They tend to branch fairly low, but the main branches grow up to carry the spreading crown well aloft.
Propagation Easy, from seed sown in spring.

RED OAK
Grevillea banksii
Fast growing, evergreen tree, flowering in spring to summer.
The red oak is a small, bushy tree; stake young plants to encourage them to grow up rather than out and remove

lower branches as needed. It usually develops a picturesque, asymmetrical habit—don't try too hard to correct it. Make cuts back to a shoot, a leaf or a lateral; grevilleas don't sprout well from bare wood.
Propagation Easy, by half-ripe cuttings in summer. Some layer well, and all can be grown easily from spring-sown seed, but seedlings may not come true as they interbreed very freely.

REDWOOD, sequoia
Sequoia
Fairly fast growing, evergreen coniferous trees, random branching type.
The only pruning either *S. sempervirens*, the Californian redwood, or the giant sequoia *S. gigantea* (*Sequoiadendron giganteum*) needs is correction of a double leader should a young tree develop one. You can remove the lower branches as the tree matures if you want to walk under it: the best time is in late winter. In its native California, but rarely here, *S. sempervirens* is sometimes used as a tall formal hedge and trimmed in late spring as the new growth develops.
Propagation Fairly easy, from spring or autumn sown seed; *S. sempervirens* can also be grown from half-ripe cuttings in summer.

ROWAN, mountain ash
Sorbus
Fairly slow growing, deciduous trees, flowering in spring.
Rowans are similar to hawthorns, and can be treated the same.
Propagation Easy, by seed in autumn (germination often waits for spring) or softwood cuttings in summer. Selected, named varieties are normally budded during summer onto seedling rootstock.

SHE-OAK
Casuarina
Fast growing, evergreen trees.
Allow young trees to grow naturally for a couple of years, then remove lower branches to raise the crown if desired. Established trees can take fairly heavy pruning but rarely need it—removal of dead or damaged branches (at any time) should be all that is necessary for these trees.
Propagation Easy. Normally from seed sown in autumn or spring, but cuttings of half-ripe wood will strike fairly readily in sand.

SILK TREE
Albizia julibrissin
Fast growing, deciduous tree, flowering in summer.
The silk tree normally grows with several trunks and can be trained to a single stem by removing all but the strongest shoot and pinching back the side shoots until the leader has reached a height of 2 m or so. Or allow it to develop naturally, merely removing crossing or crowded branches. Prune in winter or in late summer, after bloom, and take special care not to leave stubs; they will rot and infect the living branches.
Propagation Easy, from seed sown in spring.

SILKY OAK
Grevillea robusta
Fast growing, evergreen tree, flowering in spring to summer.
The silky oak needs little pruning but give young trees the usual training to establish a clean trunk and well-placed limbs. The wood is rather brittle, and so take out the weaker branches of trees in exposed positions to lessen their wind resistance. Make your cuts back to a shoot, a lateral or a leaf as it won't sprout well

from bare wood, and try not to cut large branches as it is slow to heal wounds.
Propagation Easy, by half-ripe cuttings in summer. Some layer well, and all can be grown easily from spring-sown seed, but seedlings may not come true.

SPRUCE
Picea
Slow growing, coniferous trees, whorl branching.
Spruces are naturally symmetrical growers and should need no pruning. If a young plant develops a double leader, cut the weaker out before it has a chance to spoil the tree's shape; and head any over-long branches back to a lateral. Don't cut into bare wood.
Propagation Easy, from spring-sown seed. Seed saved from blue spruces should give a proportion of blue-leaved seedlings, but selected forms such as 'Kosteriana' are usually grafted in spring on seedling stock. This isn't easy and accounts for their high price.

SWAMP CYPRESS
Taxodium distichum
Fast growing, deciduous, coniferous tree, random branching.
The only pruning likely to be needed is if a young tree develops two leaders—remove the weaker. Occasionally you may need to remove a dead branch or shorten an over-long one, but usually the tree is shapely enough. Prune in winter.
Propagation Easy, from seed or almost-ripe cuttings taken in autumn.

TREE OF HEAVEN
Ailanthus altissima, syn. *A. glandulosa*
Fast growing, deciduous tree.
A prohibited weed in some areas because of its prolific seeding and suckering, this is a

handsome tree, outstandingly tolerant of city pollution. It benefits from regular thinning of the crown to enhance its shape and make it more resistant to wind; its branches are rather brittle. Remove suckers as they appear.
Propagation Very easy, from seed in spring.

TRUMPET TREE
Tabebuia
Fast growing, mostly deciduous trees, flowering in summer.
These spectacular tropical trees need only routine pruning in youth; you can grow them either on one trunk or several. If they become lop-sided as they mature, shorten the over-long branches back to a strong lateral in autumn.
Propagation Fairly easy, by air-layering in spring or half-ripe cuttings in summer.

TULIP TREE
Liriodendron
Fairly slow growing, deciduous trees, flowering in summer.
This giant tree can't be kept small without ruining it. Watch young trees for double leaders, removing the weaker, but otherwise no pruning should be needed. If you want to take out a branch, do it early, as the tree heals large cuts only slowly. Best pruning time is winter.
Propagation Easy, from seed sown as soon as it is ripe in autumn. Variegated-leaved forms are budded in late summer on seedling understocks.

UMBRELLA TREE
Brassaia actinophylla, Schefflera
Fast growing, evergreen trees, flowering in summer.
The umbrella tree makes a tall, multi-stemmed tree, the huge leaves mainly concentrated at

the ends of the branches. Reduce its size by cutting too-tall branches to the ground or to just below where you want them to leaf out; the tree rarely makes more than one new shoot from a pruning cut. Any time from spring to autumn will suit. The smaller-leaved varieties are shrubbier but will eventually become very nearly as tall; they can be treated in exactly the same way as the large-leaved trees.

Propagation Easy, by cuttings at any time during the warmer months; a too-tall indoor plant can be air-layered, but it is simpler to just cut it down.

WALNUT

Juglans regia
Slow growing, deciduous tree, flowering in spring.

Young walnuts need the usual training in their youth to establish a good, well-spaced and strong framework of branches, as they are prone to develop narrow, weak crotches. After that no pruning other than removal of dead wood is normally needed. Young trees can be sunburnt—don't be in too much of a hurry to remove unwanted side branches until the crown has begun to develop.

Propagation Fairly easy. Seedlings (sow in autumn) will eventually be successful but if you are in a hurry, bud 'Wilson's Wonder' in late spring on seedling stock.

WATTLE

Acacia
Evergreen trees and shrubs, mostly spring flowering.

Tree species such as *A. baileyana*, *A. decurrens* and *A. polyadriifolia* need only to have the dead branches that clutter up the crowns cleaned out from time to time. Shrubby types (*A. cardiophylla*, *A.*

This is blue spruce 'Kosteriana', bluer in leaf than the ordinary type.

The silk tree needs only removal of wayward branches and perhaps lower limbs.

This tulip tree at Foxglove Spires, Tilba Tilba, NSW, is still only a baby! It will grow twice as tall and three times as wide as this, losing its pyramidal outline.

Weeping willows never look so lovely as they do when reflected in water as here at Bucki, Henty, NSW. They love moisture and will send their roots a long way to find it—keep them well away from drains and sewers.

This is the black wattle, Acacia decurrens, *one of the larger and longer lived species. Like all the tribe, it tends to accumulate dead branches.*

Two wattle blossoms. TOP: Acacia longifolia. BOTTOM: A. baileyana.

pravissima, A. rubida, A. boormannii and others of their ilk) will be bushier for trimming after bloom. Don't cut into leafless wood. Most wattles are naturally short-lived, and while cutting back after flowering will prolong their lives a little, it is better to replace old, straggly (and possibly borer-ridden) plants than to attempt to rejuvenate them by doing any heavy pruning.
Propagation Easy, by seed in autumn. Seed germinates more quickly if hot water is poured over it immediately before it is sowed.

WHITE CEDAR, chinaberry
Melia
Fast growing, deciduous tree, flowering in summer.
Young trees may need training to establish a sufficient length of trunk, and you can shorten over-long branches if needed. Established trees respond to heavy pruning in late winter but normally all they need is the removal of dead branches. The wood is fairly brittle, and you may sometimes need to remove storm-damaged wood, cutting it back to a sound lateral.
Propagation Easy, from seed sown when it is ripe, during autumn months.

WILGA
Geijera parviflora
Fast growing, evergreen small tree.
This graceful, weeping tree has unimportant flowers. To enhance it, trim back any upright side shoots to a main branch, but otherwise just remove any dead or broken branches. You can prune at any time.
Propagation Fairly easy, by seed sown during autumn. Germination is fastest if you soak it in warm water first.

WILLOW
Salix
Fast growing, deciduous trees and shrubs, flowering in spring.
Most common is the weeping willow, *S. babylonica*, a graceful tree for big gardens where its greedy roots can't get at drains and paving. It needs careful training in youth to ensure its stem is tall enough, and the branches high enough, to allow it to weep undisturbed—if you have to regularly trim off branches trailing along the ground, you may end up with an ugly crinoline effect from the shoots that grew where you cut. Mature trees need only routine removal of dead or overcrowded branches. The same is true of the less common species such as the corkscrew willow (*S. matsudana* 'Tortuosa'). Willows can take heavy pruning if needed; some of the upright types such as *S. alba* are traditionally pollarded to provide long whippy shoots for basket-making. Most willows are fairly short-lived and can become dangerously brittle with age; you may need to consult a tree surgeon.
The shrubby willows such as the pussy willow (*S. caprea*) need only the regular thinning that any shrub gets, the best time being immediately after flowering for those grown for their 'pussies'. Coloured stemmed types such as *S. irrorata* are usually cut almost to the ground at the same time, to create a bush made up entirely of new shoots, which give the brightest colour.
Propagation Very easy, by hardwood cuttings in winter. Quite large branches will take root if they are put in wet soil, giving instant trees—and at almost any time they will root in a bucket of water. Layering at any time is easy, too.

WILLOW MYRTLE
Agonis
Fast growing, evergreen trees, flowering in spring.
A. flexuosa can take quite heavy pruning but usually needs only the removal of dead wood and overcrowded branches to reveal the tree's graceful, weeping lines. Prune at any time but immediately after early summer bloom is best. The upright *A. juniperina* needs no regular attention. *A. flexuosa* will make a tall, informally pruned screen.
Propagation Fairly easy, from seed in spring or cuttings, which root rather slowly, taken in summer.

YEW
Taxus
Slow growing, evergreen coniferous tree, random branching.
Yew is the classic plant for tall hedges and topiary in Britain, but it doesn't really need pruning as it is naturally shapely. A young tree may need a wayward branch headed back, and you may find the odd branch of a mature Irish yew waving out from the plant's outline. In this case, cut it off if it is short; if not, tie it back to a branch on the opposite side of the tree. This is one of the few conifers that will grow readily from bare wood but young plants intended for hedges or topiary should be clipped from the start to ensure their bushiness to the base. Trim the new growth in summer with secateurs; when the plants have reached the size and shape you want, clip with shears two or three times during summer.
Propagation Fairly easy, by layering or half-ripe cuttings (keep them shaded until they are well rooted and starting to grow) in late summer.

INDEX

**Page numbers in *italics* refer
to illustrations**

Abelia, 9, 40
Abies, *100*, 101
absinthe *see* wormwood
Abutilon, 12, 48
Acacia, 121, *122*, 123
Acalypha, 40
acanthus, 25
Acer, 110, *110*
Acmena, 106, *107*
Actinidia chinensis, 34, *35*
Aesculus, 103
African violets, 25
Agathis, 106
Agonis, 123
Ailanthus altissima, 120
A. *glandulosa*, 120
ajuga, 23
Albizia julibrissin, *8*, 120, *121*
A. *lophantha*, 91
alders, 86
Allamanda, 28
almonds, 86
Alnus, 86
Aloysia triphylla, 60
American dogwood, 97
Ampelopsis brevipedunculata, 37
angel's trumpets, 40–1, *40*
Angophora, 87
Annona, 97
Aphelandra, 84
apple box, 87
apples, 11, 19, 25, 86–7, *86*, *87*
  see also crab-apples; custard
  apples
apricots, *88*, 89
Araucaria bidwillii, 90, *91*
A. *cunninghamii*, 103, *103*
A. *heterophylla*, 111
Arbutus unedo, *104*, 105
Artemisia, 82, 84
ash, 89, 90
Aucuba japonica, 59
Australian cypress, 89
Australian fuchsia, 41
Australian heath, 41
Australian rosemary, 41
avocados, 19, 89
Azalea, 11, 12, 13, *40*, 41

bachelor's buttons, *40*, 41
bananas, 89
barberries, 41
Bauera, 50
Bauhinia, 41–2
B. *galpinii*, 41
B. *scandens*, 41
B. *variegata*, 112

bay trees, 12, 13, *88*, 89–90
bean trees *see* Indian bean
  trees
bearded irises, 22, *22*
beauty bushes, 42
beeches, 90, *91*
begonias, 25
Berberis, 41
Betula, 90
Bignonia venusta, 31
B. *violacea*, 37
birches, 12, 90
bird of paradise bush *see* pride of
  Barbados
black currants, 50
black locust, 90
blackberries, 23
bleeding heart trees, 90
bleeding heart vines, 28
blue butterfly bushes, 42
blue sky flower, 42
bluebell creeper, 12, 28
blueberries, 42, *42*
blueberry ash, 90
boobialla, 42
Boston ivy *see* Virginia creeper
bottlebrushes, 43, *43*
Bougainvillea, 12, 28, 29
Bouvardia, 42, 43
box, 13, 14, 43–4, *44*
  see also apple box
Brachychiton acerifolius, *104*, 105
B. *discolor*, 119
B. *populneus*, 106
Brachysema, 79
Brassaia actinophylla, 120–1
breath of heaven *see* diosma
broom, 44, *45*
Browallia jamesonii, 62
Brugmansia, 40–1, *40*
Brunfelsia, 62, 63–4
buckthorn, 45
Buddleia, 12, 45, *45*
bunya pines, 90, *91*
Burmese honeysuckle, 33
butterfly bushes, 42, 45
Buxus, 13, 14, 43–4, *44*

Caesalpinia, 70
calico bush *see* mountain
  laurel
Californian lilac, 45
Californian redwood, 119
Calliandra, 53
Callistemon, 43, *43*
Callitris, 89
Calluna, 55–6
Calocedrus decurrens, 105
Calodendrum capense, 91, *91*
Calonyction aculeatum, 34

Camellia, 12, 13, 22, 25, 45, 46,
  47, *47*
camphor laurels, 90–1
Campsis, 29
Canary Island date palm, *113*
cape chestnut, 91, *91*
cape honeysuckle, 12, 28, 29
cape jasmine *see* Gardenia
Cape Leeuwin wattle, 91
Carissa, 64
carob, 93
Carolina jasmine, 28
Carya illinoinensis, 115
Cassia, 92, 93
C. *bicapsularis*, 93
C. *corymbosa*, 93
C. *fistula*, *104*, 105
C. *grandis*, 115
Castanea sativa, 94
Casuarina, 120
Catalpa bignonioides, 105
Ceanothus, 45
cedar trees, 10, 12, 92, 93, 105
  see also white cedar
Cedrus, 10, 12, *92*, 93, 105
Celtis, 101–2
Ceratonia siliqua, 93
Ceratopetalum gummiferum,
  110, 111
ceratostigma, 23
Cercis, 105–6
Cestrum, 48
C. *aurantiacum*, 48
C. *elegans*, 48
C. *nocturnum*, 64
Chaenomeles, 53
Chamaecyparis, 98, 99
Chamaelaucium uncinatum,
  54, 55
cherimoya *see* custard apples
cherry laurel, 93
cherry pie, 48
cherry trees, 12, 92, 93
chestnut trees, 91, *91*, 94
  see also horse chestnut trees
Chilean jasmine, 29
Chimonanthus praecox, 82
Chinaberry *see* white cedar
Chinese elm, 98
Chinese gooseberries *see* kiwi fruit
Chinese holly, 56
Chinese lanterns, 48
Chinese pistache, 115
Chinese snowball trees, *78*
Chinese tallow trees, 94, *95*
Chinese trumpet vine, 29
Choisya ternata, 62, 63
Christmas bush, New South
  Wales, 110, 111
Cinnamomum camphora, 90–1

Cissus, 34
Cistus, 72, 73
Citharexylum spinosum, 99
Citrus, 94, *95*
Clematis, 21, 30–1, *30*
Clerodendrum thomsoniae, 28
C. ugandense, 42
Clytostoma callistegioides, 37
Codiaeum variegatum, 49
Coleonema pulchrum, 50
coleus, 24
Convulvulus, 48, 49
Coprosma, 48
C. kirkii, 48
C. repens, 63
coral trees, 94
corkscrew willow, 123
Cornus, 50, *51*, 97
C. alba, 50
C. capitata, 97
C. chinensis, 97
C. florida, 51
Correa, 41
Corylus, 102–3, *103*
Cotinus coggygria, 78
Cotoneaster, 9, 13, 48
cotton lavender *see* lavender
    cotton
cow itch tree *see* Norfolk Island
    hibiscus
crab-apples, 94, *96*, 97
Crataegus, 102, *102*
crepe myrtle, 49, *49*
crotons, 49
crown of thorns, 50
Cryptomeria japonica, 105
Cupressocyparis leylandii, 106
Cupressus, 97
currants, 50, *51*, 53
custard apples, 97
Cydonia oblonga, 119
Cyphomandra betacea, 81, *81*
cypress trees, 10, 13, 97, 106, *107*
    see also Australian cypress; false
    cypress; swamp cypress;
    tamarisk
Cytisus, 44, *45*

daffodils, 25
Dais cotinifolia, 70
daisy bushes, 50
Daphne, 9, 50, *51*
date palm *see* Canary Island date
    palm
dawn redwood, 97
daylilies, 22
Delonix regia, 118
Deutzia, 82
diosma, 50
Diospyros kaki, 115
Dizygotheca elegantissima, 99
Dodonaea, 56
dog roses, 50
dogwood, 50, *51*, 97
Dombeya, 50–1
Duranta repens, 42

Elaeocarpus reticulatus, 90
elders, 51, 84
Eleagnus, 64, 67
elm trees, 12, 96, 97–8
    see also Japanese elm
emu bushes, 51
English hawthorns, 102
English holly, 56
Epacris, 41
Eremophilia, 51
Erica, 55–6, *55*
E. mediterranea, 55
Eriobotrya japonica, 106–7
Eriostemon, 82
E. myoporoides, 82
Erythrina, 94
Escallonia, 52
E. virgata, 52
Eucalyptus, 98–9, *98*
Euonymus, 79
Euphorbia milii, 50
E. pulcherrima, 68
evergreen magnolias, 52
Exochorda, 68

Fagus, 90, *91*
false acacia, 90
false aralia, 99
false cypress, 98, 99
false sarsaparilla, 31
Fatsia japonica, 58–9
Feijoa sellowiana, 68
Ficus, 99–101, *100*
fiddlewood, 99
fig trees, 99–101, *100*
filbert *see* hazel
fir trees, 10, *100*, 101
fire bushes, 53
firethorns, *52*, 53
firewheel trees, 101
flamboyant tree *see* poinciana
flame creeper, 31
flame trees see Illawarra flame
    trees
floor of the sky, 53
flowering cherries, 93
flowering currants, *52*, 53
flowering cypress *see*
    tamarisk
flowering maples *see* Chinese
    lanterns
flowering quinces, 13, 53
Forsythia, *52*, 53
Fortunella, 94
frangipani, *100*, 101
    see also native frangipani
Fraxinus, 89
fruit salad plant, 31
fuchsias, 12, 41, *52*, 53–4

Gardenia, 12, 54, *54*
Garrya elliptica, 78
Geijera parviflora, 123
Gelsemium sempervirens, 28
Genista see broom
Geraldton wax flower, 54, *55*

germander, 54
Gingko biloba, 108, *108*
gladioli, 22
Gleditsia triacanthos, 103
golden chain tree, *100*, 101
golden chalice vine, 31
golden elm, 97
golden rain tree, 101
Gordonia axillaris, 101
grape, 7, 25, *30*, 31, 32, 33
    see also Oregon grape
Grevillea, 9, 12, 14, 54–5, *54*
G. banksii, 119
G. biternata, 55
G. gaudichaudii, 55
G. juniperina, 55
G. robusta, 12, 55, 120
G. rosmarinifolia, 55
guava, 55, 68
guinea flowers, 33

hackberry trees, 101–2
Hakea, 55
Hardenbergia, 31
hawthorn, 57, 102, *102*
hazel, 102–3, *103*
heath, 55–6, *55*
heather, 55–6, *55*
Hebe, 81–2
Hedera, 33–4, *35*
Heliotropium, 48
Hibbertia, 33
Hibiscus, 12, 13, 56, *57*, 111
Hoheria, 59
holly, 56, *57*
honey locust trees, 103
honeysuckle, 28, *29*, 33, *33*
hoop pine, 103, *103*
hop bushes, 56
horse chestnut trees, 103
Hoya, 33, *33*
Hydrangea, 56–7, *57*
Hymenosporum flavum, *110*, 111
Hypericum, 9, 77, *77*

Ilex, 56
Illawarra flame trees, *104*, 105
incense cedar trees, 105
Indian bean trees, 105
Indian coral trees, 94
Indian hawthorn, 57
Indian laburnum, *104*, 105
Indigofera, 57
Ipomoea alba, 34
irises, bearded, 22, *22*
Irish strawberry trees, *104*, 105
Italian buckthorn, 45
Italian cypress, 97
ivy, 9, 23, 33–4, *35*
Ixora, 12, 57–8

Jacaranda mimosifolia, *104*, 105
jade plants, 58
Japanese apricot, 89
Japanese aralia, 58–9
Japanese cedar, 105

Japanese cherries, 93
Japanese elm, 105
Japanese laurel, 59
Japanese maple, *110*
Japanese pear, 114
Japanese privet, 71
jasmine, 12, 28–9, 34, *36*, 37, 59,
    66, 67
Jasminum, 34, 59
Jerusalem sage, 59
jessamine, night-scented, 64
Judas trees, 105–6
Juglans regia, 121
Juniperus, 9, 10, *10*, 59
Justicia carnea, 59

Kalmia, 64, 65
kangaroo paw, 25
kangaroo vine, 34
kauri, 106
Kerria japonica, *40*, 41
kiwi fruit, 34, *35*
Koelreuteria, 101
Kolkwitzia amabilis, 42
kowhai, 106
kurrajong, 106

Laburnum, *100*, 101
    see also Indian laburnum
lacebark, 59
    see also Queensland lacebark
lacquer palm, *112*
lad's love see wormwood
Lagerstroemia indica, 49, *49*
L. speciosa, 71
Lagunaria patersonii, 111
Lantana, 12–13, *58*, 59–60
lasiandras, 60, *61*
Lathyrus, 20, 36, 37
laurels, 59, 64, 65, 90–1
    see also bay trees; cherry laurel
Laurus nobilis, *88*, 89–90
Lavandula, 7, 13, 60, *61*
lavender, 7, 13, 60, *61*
lavender cotton, 60
leadwort, 60
Lechenaultia biloba, 53
lemon scented verbena, 60
Leptospermum, 79–80, *80*
lettuce, 19
Leucospermum, 60, *61*
Leyland cypress, 106
Ligustrum, 71
lilac, 60, *61*, 62
    see also Californian lilac
lillypilly, 106, *107*
Linodendron, 120, *121*
Lippia citriodora, 60
Liquidambar, 106
Liriodendron, 120
Litchi chinensis, 107
Lombardy poplar, *118*
London plane tree, *117*
Lonicera, 33, *33*
loquat trees, 106–7
Loropetalum chinense, 62

Luculia, 62
lychees, 107

Macadamia, 107–8
Magnolia, 108, *108*, *109*
magnolias, 8, 52, 70, 108, *108*, *109*
Mahonia, 66, 67
maidenhair trees, 108, *108*
maid's ruin see wormwood
Malus, 94, 96, 97
M. cultivars, 86–7, *86*, *87*
Mandevilla, 12, 29
M. laxa, 29
Mangifera indica, 108, *108*, 110
mangoes, 108, *108*, 110
maple, 110, *110*
marigolds, 7, 22
marmalade bushes, 62–3
may, 63
    see also hawthorn
Melaleuca, 67–8
Melia, 123
Metasequoia glyptostroboides, 97
Mexican orange blossom, 62, 63
Michelia, 52
M. champaca, 52
M. doltsopa, 52
M. figo, 70
M. yunnanensis, 52
Mickey Mouse plants, 63
mirror plants, 63
mock orange, 62, 63
mock violets see *Buddleia davidii*
Monstera deliciosa, 31
Monterey cypress, 97
moonflower, 34
Moreton Bay fig tree, 99
morning-noon-and-night, 62, 63–4
Morus, 110–11, *110*
mountain ash see rowan
mountain laurel, 64, *65*
Muehlenbeckia axillaria, 77
mulberry trees, 110–11, *110*
Murraya paniculata, 66, 67
Musa, 89
Myoporum, 42
myrtle, 49, *49*, 64, *65*
    see also willow myrtle
Myrtus communis, 64, 65

Nandina domestica, 76–7, *77*
nashi, 114
nasturtiums, 20
Natal plums, 64
native frangipani, *110*, 111
nectarines, 112–13, *113*
Nerium, 64, 65
New South Wales Christmas bush,
    110, 111
night-scented jessamine, 64
Norfolk Island hibiscus, 111
Norfolk Island pine, 111

oak trees, 111
    see also red oak trees; she-oaks
Ochna serrulata, 63

Olea europaea, 111–12
oleander, 13, 64, 65, 84
Olearia, 50
oleaster, 64, 67
olive trees, 111–12
Omalanthus populifolius, 90
orange blossom see Mexican
    orange blossom
orange jasmine, 66, 67
orange trees, 94
orchid trees, 112
orchids, 25
Oregon grape, 66, 67
ornamental fig see fig trees
Osmanthus, 66, 67

Paeonia suffruticosa, 80–1, *80*
pagoda trees, 112
palm trees, 112, *112*, 113
Pandorea, 38
paperbark, 67–8
Parthenocissus, 35, 37–8
Passiflora, 36
passionfruit, 36
Paulownia, 119
P. tomentosa, 25
peach trees, 112–13, *113*
pear trees, 11, 25, 113–14,
    113, *114*
pearl bushes, 68
pecan trees, 115
pencil pines see cypress trees
peonies, *22*, 25
    see also tree peonies
pepper trees, *114*, 115
Persea americana, 89
persimmon trees, 115
petunias, 7, 22
Philadelphus, 9, 11, 62, 63
Phlomis, 59
phlox, 25
Photinia, 68
Picea, 120, *121*
Pieris, 68
pigeon berry see blue sky flower
pine trees, 10, *10*, 90, *91*, 103,
    103, 111, *114*, 115
pineapple guava, 68
pink shower, 115
Pinus, *114*, 115
pistachio trees, 115–16
Pistacia, 115–16
Pittosporum, *4*, 116
plane trees, 116, *117*
Platanus, 116, *117*
Plumbago auriculata, 60
Plumeria, *100*, 101
plums, 116
    see also Natal plums
Podocarpus, 10, 118
poinciana, 118
poinsettia, 11, 68, *69*
Polygala, 79
pomegranates, 69, *69*
pompon bushes, 70
poplar trees, 118–19, *118*

poplar trees, Queensland *see* bleeding heart trees
Populus, 118–19, *118*
Portulacaria afra, 58
portwine magnolias, 70
potato vine, 36–7
powder-puff bush *see* fire bushes
powton *see* princess tree
pride of Barbados, 70
pride of India *see* crepe myrtle
princess trees, 25, 119
privet, 13, 14, 71
Prunus, 92, 93
P. armeniaca, 89
P. avium, 93
P. cerasifera, 116
P. domestica, 116
P. dulcis, 86
P. glandulosa, 93
P. laurocerasus, 93
P. lusitanica, 93
P. mume, 89
P. persica cultivars, 112–13, *113*
P. serrulata, 93
P. subhirtella, 92
Psidium, 55
pumpkins, 20
Punica granatum, 69, *69*
pussy willow, 123
Pyracantha, 52, 53
pyramid tree *see* Norfolk Island hibiscus
Pyrostegia venusta, 31
Pyrus, 113–14

queen's flowers, 71
Queensland lacebark, 119
Queensland nut *see Macadamia*
Queensland poplar *see* bleeding heart trees
Quercus, 111
quinces, 13, 53, 119
Quisqualis indica, 37

rain trees, 101, 119
Rangoon creeper, 37
Raphiolepis, 12, 57
raspberries, 71
red oak trees, 119
redbud *see* Judas trees
redwood trees, 97, 119
Rhamnus, 45
Rhododendron, 18, 24, 40, 70, 71–2
Ribes, 50, 52, 53
rice-paper plants, 72, 73
river roses *see* dog roses
Robinia, 90
rock roses, 72, 73
Romneya coulteri, 25
Rondeletia amoena, 72, 73
rose of sharon, 56
rosemary, 13, 41, 76, 77
roses, 7, 9, 11, 12, 13, 19, 22, 23, 26, *26*, 50, 72–3, *73*, 74, 75–6, *75*, 76

Rosmarinus officinalis, 76
rowan, 119
rubber trees *see* fig trees
Rubus idaeus, 70

sacred bamboo, 76–7, *77*
sage, Jerusalem, 59
Saint John's wort, 77, *77*
Salix, *122*, 123
Samanea saman, 119
Sambucus, 51
Santolina chamaecyparissus, 60
Sapium sebiferum, 94, *95*
Schefflera, 120–1
Schinus ariera, 115
Sequoia, 10, 119
she-oaks, 120
silk tassel bush, 78
silk trees, 8, 120, *121*
silky oak, 55, 120
silver pear, 114
sky flowers, 37
smoke bush, 78
snowball trees, 78–9, *78*
snowberries, 23, 79
Solandra maxima, 31
Solanum, 36–7
S. jasminoides, 12, 36
S. wendlandii, 36
Sollya heterophylla, 12, 28
Sophora japonica, 112
S. tetraptera, 106
Sorbus, 119
Spartium see broom
spindle trees, 79
Spiraea, 63
spotted laurel *see* Japanese laurel
spruce, 10, 120, *121*
spurge laurel *see Daphne*
star jasmine, 12, 36, 37
Stenocarpus sinuatus, 101
Stenolobium stans see Tecoma stans
strawberries, 23
strawberry trees *see* Irish strawberry tree
Streptosolen jamesonii, 62–3
sugarberry *see* hackberry trees
swamp cypress, 120
Swan River pea bushes, 79
sweet-pea bushes, 79
sweet peas, 20, 36, 37
sweetshade *see* native frangipani
Symphoricarpos, 23, 79
Syringa, 60, *61*, 62

Tabebuia, 120
tallow trees *see* Chinese tallow trees
tamarillo *see* tree tomatoes
tamarisk, 79
Tamarix, 79
Taxodium distichum, 120
Taxus, 10, 123
tea tree, 79–80, *80*
Tecoma stans, 84

Tecomaria capensis, 12, 28, 29
Telopea, 82, *83*
Tetrapanax papyrifera, 72, 73
Teucrium, 54
Thevetia, 84
Thunbergia, 37
thyme, creeping, 80, *80*
Thymus, 80, *80*
Tibouchina, 60
tomatoes, tree, 81, *81*
Trachelospermum jasminoides, 12, 36, 37
tree-in-a-hurry *see* Cape Leeuwin wattle
tree of heaven, 120
tree peonies, 80–1, *81*
tree tomatoes, 81, *81*
trumpet trees, 120
trumpet vines, 29, 37
tulip trees, 120, *121*
turquoise berry vine, 37

Ulmus, 96, 97–8
umbrella trees, 120–1

Vaccinium, 42
verbena, lemon scented, 60
veronica, 81–2
Viburnum, 82
V. macrocephalum, 78
V. opulus, 78–9
vinca, 9
Virginia creeper, 35, 37–8
Vitis heterophylla, 37
V. vinifera, 30, 31, 32, 33

walnut trees, 121
waratahs, 82, *83*
wattle trees, 121, *122*, 123
see also Cape Leeuwin wattle
wax flowers, 82
wedding bells, 82
weeping cherries, 92
weeping willows, *122*, 123
Weigela, 11, 82, 84
Westringia, 41
white cedar, 123
wig trees, 78
wilga, 123
willow-leaved pear, 114
willow myrtle, 123
willow pattern tree *see* golden rain tree
willow trees, *122*, 123
wintersweet, 82
Wisteria, 4, 11, 12, 25, 38, *38*
wonga-wonga vine, 38
woolum *see* native frangipani
wormwood, 82, *84*

yellow elder, 84
yellow oleander, 84
yew, 10, 13, 14, 123

zebra plant, 84
Zelkova, 105

Published by Murdoch Books®, a division of Murdoch Magazines Pty Limited
213 Miller Street, North Sydney NSW 2060

Designer: Marylouise Brammer
Editor: Christine Eslick
Illustrations: Helen McCosker
Photographs: *Better Homes and Gardens Picture Library*: 10, 11 left and right,
13, 20, 21, 22, 24, 29 top, 33 left;
Kim Brun Photography: front cover;
Geoffrey Burnie: 44, 46, 52 top and centre right, 55 right, 61 top right and centre left, 62 top, 69
top, 73 bottom left, 78, 80 bottom, 83, 100 centre right, 104 top centre, 110 bottom;
Leigh Clapp: 61 top left, 92 right, 98 bottom;
Densey Clyne: 36 top, 52 centre left, 54 right, 57 centre, 61 centre right, 62 centre, 65 bottom, 74
top left and right and bottom right, 84 top, 91 top right and bottom, 103 right,
104 top left, 108 left, 110 centre left and right, 122 bottom left and right
Stirling Macoboy: 19 top, 35 left, 36 bottom, 43, 61 bottom left,
62 bottom right, 74 bottom left, 121 top left;
Lorna Rose: 1, 3 bottom, 30 top and bottom, 35 right, 39, 40 centre and bottom,
42, 47, 49 top, 51 centre, 57 bottom, 58, 66 top and bottom left and right,
69 bottom left, 73 top and centre, 77 centre and bottom, 81, 87, 88, 91 top left, 95
top right and bottom right, 96 bottom left, 98 top, 100 top and bottom left, 102, 103 left, 104
top right and bottom, 107 top, 108 centre and right, 109, 112 left, 113 bottom,
114 centre and bottom, 118, 121 bottom, 122 top;
Gerry Whitmont: 3 top and centre, 18, 27, 33 right, 49 bottom, 51 top, 52 bottom,
54 left, 55 left, 65 top, 70 top, 80 top right, 84 bottom, 85, 86, 92 bottom left,
96 top, 107 bottom, 114 top left, 117, 122 centre right, inside front cover, back cover;
Terry Williams: 4, 6, 17, 26, 29 bottom, 73 bottom right, 95 bottom left, 113 top right;
Brett and Susan Wright: 2, 40 top

Publisher: Anne Wilson
Publishing Manager: Mark Newman
Managing Editor: Susan Tomnay
Art Director: Lena Lowe
Production Manager: Catie Ziller
Marketing Manager: Mark Smith
National Sales Manager: Keith Watson
Photo Librarian: Dianne Bedford

National Library of Australia
Cataloguing-in-Publication data
Mann, Roger, 1948–
Pruning and Planting.
Includes index.
ISBN 0 86411 371 4.
1. Plant propagation. 2. Pruning. I. Title.
635.9153

Printed by Prestige Litho, Qld

Australian distribution to supermarkets and newsagents by Gordon & Gotch Ltd,
68 Kingsgrove Road, Belmore NSW 2192

*Better Homes and Gardens® (Trade Mark) Regd T.M. of Meredith Corporation

Front cover: Climbing rose **Back cover:** Hydrangeas
Title page: Box hedging **Page 2:** Azaleas **Page 3** top: *Cornus caputata,* evergreen dogwood;
centre: Waratah; bottom: *Aphelandra* and coleus leaves